CHRISTIAN MERCY

Compassion, Proclamation, and Power

D. Thompson

DEDICATION

*I dedicate this book to my father-in-law Archie Mitchell,
Dr. Ardelle Vietti, Dan Gerber, and Ruth Wilting, all of whom
were killed by Communist forces in Viet Nam after 1962.*

*They gave their lives to care for the thousands of leprosy
patients living as outcasts in the forests and mountains of
central Viet Nam.*

*Their willingness to risk everything to help these despised
and suffering people and introduce them to Jesus illustrates
everything that Jesus taught about mercy.*

Acknowledgements

I could not have written this book without the encouragement of my wife, Rebecca, who for more than three decades has worked at my side in Africa caring for the sick and demonstrating to her students how God calls us to care for them.

I am deeply indebted to my editors, James Watkins and Shirley Biggers, for working so patiently with me and turning my stumbling grammar and syntax into something readable and clear.

My good friend Bill Giovannetti, the senior pastor of the Neighborhood Church of Redding, California, probably did more to help me get this book ready for publication than anyone else. He insisted that *Christian Mercy* is a book the American Church needs to have and prodded me again and again until I finished it. He also provided me with priceless practical advice.

Finally, and most importantly, I want to thank the Lord Jesus, since he is the one who taught me everything I know about helping suffering people. Again and again he reminded me of his words and his example as he cared for suffering people, and gently corrected me when I was selfish, proud, and uncaring.

TABLE OF CONTENTS

The quality of mercy is not strain'd,
It droppeth as the gentle rain from heaven
Upon the place beneath, it is twice blest;
It blesseth him that gives, and him that takes:

William Shakespeare
The Merchant of Venice
Act 4, scene 1

FOREWORD

The world has no shortage of those who would do good. Western society embraces the idea of giving back and paying it forward. Celebrities, athletes, politicians, and would-be do-gooders vie for high profile opportunities to make the world a better place.

Thank God for this impulse to help the less fortunate. I take it as the image of God at work—a tiny fraction of his infinite benevolence still asserting itself in fallen human nature.

Even so, no amount of societal improvement can send a soul to heaven. If we claim to be heirs of Jesus, and if we follow the Christian message, we cannot help but look beyond the horizons of this mortal life to an everlasting world above. God has set eternity in our hearts, said wise King Solomon. We will live forever either with or without God.

That reality defines every aspect of the Christian mission.

Christianity offers the world immeasurably more than Oprah with a little Jesus sprinkled on top. It offers a gospel of forgiveness, a life of supernatural grace, and a hereafter in the presence of a God at whose right hand are pleasures evermore. We believe in the love of God for time *and* eternity, not one or the other, but both.

My friend, D. Thompson, offers a much-needed corrective for today's diminished Christian message. He calls us to alleviate suffering *and* to summon people to Christ. We are to do good, he says, but we must do more than good: we must also invite a hungry world to the gospel feast.

In the words of an old Baptist preacher: "I don't care how much good you do, if your church is not getting people saved, you're not Christian."

Dr. Thompson has earned the right to speak on this subject. A lifetime of medical mission work among the poorest of the poor— and with that, a lifetime of telling people about the eternal Savior, Jesus—makes him uniquely qualified to call the church to her truest mercy. May God use *Christian Mercy* to reawaken God's people to the priority of true evangelism: the proclamation of the gospel of Christ crucified, in the power of the Holy Spirit, wrapped up in the self-giving love of the Church.

Dr. Bill Giovannetti
Pastor, Professor, Author
California, 2013

INTRODUCTION

A merican churches have been riding a pendulum for more than one hundred years, and the pendulum is swinging again: from a theology that strongly emphasizes the importance of proclaiming the gospel and at times neglects mercy and justice to a theology that prizes compassion, neglects proclamation, and is almost silent about miracles of healing and deliverance.

The majority of recent books published on the subject of mercy and compassion rightly calls on American Christians to do more to help the poor, feed the hungry, and stand for justice. This emphasis can leave readers with the unintended impression that the gospel equals "peace and justice on earth." In *What is the Mission of the Church*,[1] Kevin DeYoung and Greg Gilbert write, "We are concerned that in all our passion for renewing the city or tackling social problems, we run the risk of marginalizing the one thing that makes Christian mission Christian: namely, making disciples of Jesus Christ."

But are we again laying the groundwork for a return to the "social gospel" of 1900-1960 that closed the hearts of American evangelicals to suffering people for one hundred years? By leaving out the teachings of Christ about healing and deliverance, are we returning to an intellectualized and sterile gospel?

The apostle Paul wrote in Romans 1:16, "For I am not ashamed of this Good News about Christ. It is the power of God at work, saving everyone who believes. . . ." He concluded in verse 17 with the statement, "It is through *faith* that a righteous person has life" (*emphasis* mine).

What exactly is *Christian* mercy? Is it simply what Christians today are doing to help the sick, the hungry, the homeless, and the poor? Is it another ideal we should aspire to? In this book I will build the argument that *Christian Mercy is what Jesus taught and modeled.* Jesus combined his acts of love with the *spoken gospel,* with *spiritual power* and with *faith. His* mercy freed people who were enslaved by sin, who were sick, who were hungry and in despair, and moved them to freedom, health, joy, and life. This is the kind of mercy our world needs today, and anything less is a pale, weak imitation.

In talking about mercy, DeYoung and Gilbert don't mince words about the importance of the spoken gospel:

We want to make sure the gospel—the good news of Christ's death for sin and subsequent resurrection—is of first importance in our churches. We want the crystal-clear and utterly unique task of the church—making disciples of Jesus Christ to the glory of God the Father—put front and center, not lost in a flurry of commendable concerns. We want the church to remember that there is something worse than death and something better than human flourishing. We believe the church is sent into the world to witness to Jesus by proclaiming the gospel and making disciples of all nations. This is our task. This is our unique and central calling. We strongly support mercy ministries, and we must understand these endeavors in the right theological categories without sacrificing more explicit priorities. "[2]

But simply balancing compassion ministries with proclamation will not be enough to bring us in line with Jesus' teachings and example: there must also be a *power* in our proclamation and in our healing that is stronger than human effort—the same power Jesus demonstrated when he healed, raised the dead, and cast out evil spirits. If we are to follow Jesus we cannot and must not exclude miracles.

Christians serving in compassion ministries need a balanced biblical theology to inspire and guide them. Misleading humanitarian manifestos—the latest reaction to the perceived failures of the previous generation of Christians and proclamation without spiritual power—can never measure up to the model Jesus gave. Unless we base our mercy on the solid rock of Jesus, we will ride a pendulum between the extremes of humanitarianism without the gospel and a loveless gospel without power.

This is the central message of *Christian Mercy*. It is written for the average Christian, centered on the teachings and example of Jesus, explained in modern terms, and made practical for our time with real life stories from my thirty-five years of experience as a missionary surgeon serving among the poor in Africa.

D. Thompson
January, 2013

Chapter 1
TRUE MERCY

Most of our brothers and sisters in Christ in the developing world
live in grinding poverty. And in the midst of this stands the Church
of Jesus Christ in America, with resources, knowledge, and tools
unequaled in the history of Christendom. I believe that we stand on
the brink of a defining moment. We have a choice to make. [3]

Mercy Snapshots

In a hospital in one of the driest countries in West Africa, I photographed a sad and dejected five-year-old girl slumped on a plain wooden bench. Her right arm lay swollen, blistered, and useless against her side. She sat perfectly still, but her red-rimmed eyes betrayed her pain. Ten days earlier, she had fallen and broken her arm. Her father, a subsistence corn farmer, took her to the village bonesetter. He placed wooden slats around her broken forearm to serve as a splint and then bound it tightly in place. But he made the splint so tight that it cut off the circulation and caused her hand to swell. She tried to be brave and endure, but the pain was beyond endurance. That night she cried and even screamed, but the village bonesetter refused to take the splint off, insisting that the pain would soon diminish. The next morning the pain did go away, much to her parents' relief. But their little girl's hand had swelled to twice its normal size and she no longer had feeling in her fingers. A few days later blisters appeared on her wrist, so her father cut off the splint. What he saw convinced him to take her to the hospital.

Early in the next morning while it was still dark, he and his daughter climbed on a bus that was going in the direction of Galmi hospital. They arrived an hour later and waited with hundreds of other patients for the gates to open. The guard opened the gate at 8 o'clock, and the crowd nearly stampeded. Seeing the little girl's condition, the guard made sure she was one of those admitted. An hour later, she was registered and taken to the waiting area. A nurse came down the row to see who needed emergency treatment, and when he saw her arm, motioned her father to bring his daughter to the surgery clinic.

When it was their turn, a doctor came into the examining room wearing a white coat over what looked like blue pajamas. As he examined the little girl's arm, his eyes were sad and kind. He did not seem surprised that she could not feel anything when he touched her swollen hand. A minute later, I walked into the room and took the little girl's picture.

Her arm was dead below the elbow. An X-ray revealed fractures of the bones in her forearm, but the fractures were minor compared to the damage the bonesetter had caused. That afternoon the surgeon, who had traveled ten thousand miles at his own expense to volunteer his skills for a month, amputated her arm below the elbow.

The next morning, I saw a five-year-old boy lying comatose in the ICU ward, his head bandaged. His grandmother sat on a chair next to the bed, her hand on her grandson's leg. She was hoping that he would wake up. Two days earlier, he had fallen down a thirty-foot well while trying to pull up a bucket of water. He didn't look like as if he even weighed twenty pounds, and the thought of this skinny little preschooler hauling a bucket of water up from the bottom of a thirty-foot well sounded bizarre. Somewhere on his way to the bottom of the well the little guy hit his head, cut his scalp, and caved in part of his cranium. Why he hadn't drowned or died instantly was a mystery.

The family rushed the boy to the hospital, where another volunteer surgeon took the injured boy to the operating room, cleaned out the wound, and levered the bone fragment up so it was no longer pressing on the brain. The nurses and the boy's grandmother watched over him all night, but the next morning he still had not awakened. All that day, everyone prayed that he would survive. The second morning, as I made rounds with the surgeon, the boy surprised us all and opened his eyes!

In the joy of that moment, the wonder of his improbable treatment by a volunteer surgeon from America was briefly forgotten. Only later came the realization that the gifts of mercy bestowed on that young boy were given because God had radically changed the hearts of these skilled doctors and had called them to be merciful.

Why Have Mercy?

For the follower of Jesus, there are at least four reasons to be merciful to others. The first is that *God is merciful to us.* Jesus told a parable about a servant who owed the king a great deal of money. When the king threatened to imprison him until he paid off the loan, the servant fell on his knees and begged for mercy. The king had pity on him and forgave him his entire debt. Afterward, the servant went to one of the other servants and demanded that he pay him what he owed. When his fellow servant begged for mercy, the forgiven servant threw him in prison instead. When the king heard what the servant he had pardoned had done to his colleague, he was furious. So he reinstated the unmerciful man's debt and threw *him* into prison!

In this story, Jesus makes the point that unless we are merciful and forgive others, God will withdraw his mercy and will not forgive us. In other words, "what goes around comes around"—not just in the life to come, but in this life too. Today we may be physically strong and have resources at our disposal to help others, but someday it will be our turn to be weak and needy. This is what Jesus was talking about when he said to his disciples in Matthew 5:7, "God blesses those who are merciful, for they will be shown mercy."

At the height of his ministry, the apostle Peter healed thousands of people. In the city of Caesarea people laid the sick where Peter would pass, and even if his shadow touched them, they were healed. Yet Jesus told him that at the end of his life he would be so feeble that someone would have to dress him. Old age and sickness awaits all of us, and unless Jesus returns before then, not one of us will escape death. If we are merciful to others, God will make sure that others show mercy to us.

The second reason to have mercy on others is that the *triune God is merciful.* Instead of destroying the entire human race for continually disobeying him, God decided to send the Son to earth as a human being. In all of history there will never be an act of mercy so great and so costly as Jesus offering of himself to suffer and die on the cross for our sins, and the Father and the Holy Spirit's willingness to help him accomplish it.

The third and most important reason for you as a follower of Jesus to have mercy on others is because *God's very DNA is inside of you.* If you are a Christian, you have the Holy Spirit inside of you, and unless you resist him, mercy will come to you naturally.

A fourth reason we should have mercy on others is that until Jesus returns to earth, *"having mercy" is our mission to the world.* Not only is this God's way to bless people; it's the only way the nations of the world are going to hear about his Son Jesus.

The Holy Spirit's Work

The stories at the beginning of this chapter illustrate the steps to being compassionate. The first is *to have the capacity to perceive another person's suffering.* The second is *to feel grief* for that person's suffering. The third is to have *a heart that is free of condemnation,* and the fourth is to feel *a sense of urgency to take effective action.* All of these steps must be enabled by the work of the Holy Spirit in the heart of a believer. For selfish reasons and because of fear, many of us resist the Holy Spirit.

Some who don't believe this might say that mercy and compassion come from a pure heart. Well, a baby has a pure heart, but a baby shows no gratitude for the suffering of its mother when she gives birth. Neither does a baby notice how much effort and expense his family expends for him to grow and develop during his first years of life. From a baby's point of view, others exist to serve him. Therefore, mercy is not a natural byproduct of innocence.

According to Jesus, an important sign that someone loves God is that he places the needs of others above his own needs and finds joy in serving others. That was the point he made to his disciples on the night of his crucifixion when he knelt before each one of them and washed their feet. Afterwards he said to them, "Since I, your Lord and Teacher, have washed your feet, you ought to wash each other's feet" (John 13:14). In John 15:13 he said, "There is no greater love than to lay down one's life for one's friend." Then Jesus laid down his life for his friends.

In the history of the world, no one has exemplified mercy more clearly than Jesus, the Messiah. In Isaiah 53, the prophet Isaiah wrote about Jesus in some of the most beautiful prose ever written.

Who has believed our message? To whom has the Lord revealed his powerful arm? My servant grew up in the Lord's presence like a tender green shoot, like a root in the ground. There was nothing beautiful or majestic about his appearance, nothing to attract us to him. He was despised and rejected—a man of sorrows, acquainted with deepest grief. We turned our backs on him and looked the other way. He was despised, and we did not care. Yet it was our weaknesses he carried. It was our sorrows that weighed him down. And we thought his troubles were a punishment from God, a punishment for his own sins! But he was pierced for our rebellion, crushed for our sins. He was beaten so we could be whole. He was whipped so we could be healed. All of us, like sheep, have strayed away. We have left God's paths to follow our own. Yet the Lord laid on him the sins for us all. He was oppressed and treated harshly, yet he never said a word. He was led like a lamb to the slaughter. And as a sheep is silent before the shearers, he did not open his mouth. Unjustly condemned, he was led away. No one cared that he died without descendants, that his life was cut short in midstream. But he was struck down for the rebellion of my people. He had done no wrong and had never deceived anyone. But he was buried like a criminal; he was put in a rich man's grave. But it was the Lord's good plan to crush him and cause him grief. Yet when his life is made an offering for sin he will have many descendants. He will enjoy a long life and the Lord's good plan will prosper in his hands. When he sees all that is accomplished by his anguish he will be satisfied. And because of his experience my righteous servant will make it possible for many to be counted righteous, for he will bear all their sins. I will give him the honors of a victorious soldier, because he exposed himself to death. He was counted among the rebels. He bore the sins of many and interceded for rebels.

The wellspring of that kind of mercy—the kind that the Church needs today—is only found in God.

If we are to exemplify the mercy of Jesus, we must be willing to move beyond our own suffering and disappointments and perceive the suffering of others. But perception alone will not produce mercy. What must happen next is that we must open our hearts to *grieve* for people who suffer. The surgeons in the stories at the beginning of this chapter lived more than ten thousand miles away from the hospital in West Africa where I found them serving the sick. When they heard of the suffering of the children who were brought to this hospital and when they understood that the people they were hearing about did not know Jesus, they did not turn away. Instead, they grieved for them.

Every day of the year, we can see on our televisions and our computer screens images of people suffering. If it happens often enough, we become used to these images and can watch them without experiencing grief. Often we simply turn to a different channel. Steve Moore, in his book *Who Is My Neighbor?* calls this "pseudo-compassion fatigue." He writes,

> *As the world continues to get smaller and communication continues to get faster, we are in danger of producing a society that lives in chronic pseudo-compassion fatigue. I say pseudo-compassion fatigue because it does not result from the traditional caregiver experience of giving too much without taking time to refuel. It is the result of too much almost giving, almost serving.*[4]

Real compassion fatigue occurs to people who involve themselves so deeply in helping others under strenuous and unrelenting conditions that they became emotionally and physically exhausted. In order to recover, they need to be sheltered from suffering, to escape from stress, and to rest. Some may even require counseling and medication to recover. These are people who are grieving so deeply for those they are helping that they themselves end up needing help.

Another reason we might not grieve over the suffering of another is if we think that person deserves what he's getting. We might even secretly rejoice in his pain.

When the AIDS epidemic exploded across Africa, many Christians and churches responded with righteous indignation. Some pastors preached from their pulpits that the disease was the result of sexual promiscuity. They were right about that most of the time, except when women were infected through rape, people contracted the disease through blood transfusions, or children contracted it from their mothers during childbirth or from nursing at their mother's breast. Unfortunately, many Christians and pastors didn't stop there. They went on to say that because AIDS was God's righteous judgment, they were *exempted from all responsibility to help them.*

Timothy Lane and Pal Tripp wrote in *Relationships, A Mess Worth Making,*

> *Mercy has eyes. It pays attention to your distress and notices your weaknesses and failures. But mercy looks at these things with eyes of compassion. It doesn't criticize you for the tough situation you are in or condemn you for your sin. Mercy wants to relieve your suffering and forgive your debt.*[5]

This kind of mercy comes from the heart of God. As we shall see in later chapters, the perception of suffering and the emotion of grief are not enough. Before we can act, our hearts must be free of condemnation and judgment.

But the work of the Holy Spirit does not end there, because the awareness of suffering and the grief that occurs are still not enough to produce mercy. Before we will act, the Holy Spirit *must give us a sense of urgency to take effective action to alleviate the suffering.*

At one time or another, we have all had these feelings for others, yet we have done nothing to help them. If you have been to a desperately poor country, perhaps beggars approached you and asked you for money or food. If you grew up in America, you would have felt pity for them, especially if they were lame, had lost a hand or an eye, appeared malnourished, or were wearing rags. If you were especially tenderhearted, you might feel grief about their situation.

What usually happened next? Maybe irritation? If you were like me, the approach may have caught you by surprise. Perhaps you had only twenty-dollar bills in your pocket, much too much to hand out to a stranger. The only thing left to do was to ignore him. Besides, what would a single gift do anyway?

If you've read Steve Corbitt and Brian Fikkert's book, *When Helping Hurts,* you will know that giving out a few coins will probably not change anything for such people. Tomorrow that same beggar will still have to ask people to give him money to live on.

You might have wondered if the beggar who approached you was for hire and if there might not be someone who would collect his money and drive away in a Mercedes. I've even caught myself thinking that if I gave an obvious alcoholic enough money to buy bread he would just go buy another drink. All of these scenarios can leave us feeling irritated and upset. Obviously, perceiving another person's suffering and feeling grief for that person is not the same thing as being merciful.

James wrote about this in chapter 2:14-16: "What good is it, dear brothers and sisters, if you say you have faith but don't show it by your actions? Can that kind of faith save anyone? Suppose you see a brother or sister who has no food or clothing, and you say, 'Good-bye and have a good day; stay warm and eat well'—but then you don't give that person any food or clothing? What good does that do?"

Being merciful to those who are suffering means finding effective ways to alleviate their pain. If giving a few dollars to a beggar does not change his situation, then what will?

When the two surgeons in the stories at the beginning of this chapter heard of the suffering of the people in Niger and grieved for them, they realized that to solve the problem they would have to take radical action. One of the surgeons sold his practice, talked his church into financially backing him, and moved with his wife to live and work at SIM-Galmi Hospital in the country of Niger. The other surgeon decided to spend several months a year working at the hospital at his own expense. Since the problem in Niger is much bigger than what they could possibly handle themselves, they also participated in a long-term project to train Christian African doctors to become skilled surgeons and to serve the sick with the same mercy and compassion that God placed in their hearts.

Real mercy demands of us the capacity to perceive suffering in others, the capacity to grieve for the suffering and lostness of others, the lack in our hearts of an attitude of condemnation, and effective action.

Now we will look at how and why Christian mercy differs from church tradition and from what humanitarians are doing to help people all over the world, and why the difference is so important for the Church of Jesus Christ.

Chapter 2

WHICH MERCY?

"My thoughts are nothing like your thoughts," says the Lord. "And my ways are far beyond anything you could imagine. For just as the heavens are higher than the earth, so my ways are higher than your ways and my thoughts higher than your thoughts."

Isaiah 55:8-9

My Journey into Mercy

It might surprise you to know that even though I was a doctor, I did not know about God's kind of mercy and compassion when I first arrived in Gabon, Africa, to establish a mission hospital. Twenty years into my service at the tiny hospital my wife and I and a small band of volunteers had started, I was surprised one day to find myself in a serious argument with the African church leaders we had come to love. They were the same men and women who had invited us decades earlier to help them establish a medical work to serve the poorest people in the country.

In those early days, three out of every five children in the region died of preventable or treatable diseases. Malaria, whooping cough, measles, dysentery, and tuberculosis raged unopposed. Every year polio left thousands of children paralyzed for life. One out of thirty women died in childbirth, and one in twenty newborns did not survive the first month of life. The few government hospitals that were open had few medicines to give out and even fewer people who knew how to use them.

Before we came, the few doctors who were willing to venture out of Gabon's capital to serve in the provinces were too poorly trained and equipped to perform emergency surgery for obstructed labor, strangulated hernias, bowel obstructions, appendicitis, and major fractures. Nurses working in the interior were trained on site, barely literate, and without classrooms or textbooks. One out of every ten adults had a hernia and many of them died when their hernias became strangulated. By the early seventies, the population of Gabon was either stagnant or *declining*. Perhaps because of these reasons, of the five countries that had once made up French West Equatorial Guinea (French Congo, Gabon, Cameroon, Central African Republic, and Chad), Gabon was the least populated.

We inherited a small dispensary located in a town of just thirty-five hundred people. Our medical team consisted of one doctor (me), five missionary nurses, and one African nurse.

Twenty years later, we had built a sixty-bed hospital that provided prenatal and maternity services, surgery, gynecology, pediatrics, adult medical care, a mobile vaccination team, a public health program, a nursing school, and three satellite dispensaries. The hospital treated more than twenty thousand outpatients a year, most of whom heard the gospel in waiting areas or on the wards. By the mid 90's, thousands of them began turning to Christ. A European research firm, hired by the government to evaluate the country's health services, reported that our hospital was "the best and most cost-effective medical facility in Gabon." We were suddenly catapulted from obscurity to acclamation, and that was when the argument with the church leaders began.

In its annual synod that year, the African church leaders decided to charge the hospital ten percent of its income from patients. The church needed money, and many pastors felt that the hospital was not properly contributing to the church's expenses, even though the hospital was providing free health care for all of the church's pastors, evangelists, and their families.

If the hospital had been doing well financially we might have acquiesced, but we had set the prices very low so that even the poorest could afford to be treated. We were barely making ends meet, but we were accomplishing what the church had asked us to do. The hospital was surviving financially because our mission was paying our salaries and housing, and several other agencies were giving financial assistance. If the church took ten percent of our income we would have to cut back on our services, lay off several of our employees, and stop treating those who couldn't pay. I was unwilling to do any of these things.

The debate started on a low key but quickly rose in pitch and intensity. Both sides argued their points with growing emotion, and it quickly developed into a confrontation between Western missionaries and African church leaders. Using Western accounting financial arguments, we explained how siphoning away ten percent of the hospital's income would lead to bankruptcy, unless our donors paid more. The church leaders replied that the hospital had no authority to challenge its decision and should tithe a tenth of its income like everyone else. All over Africa, church hospitals were doing what the church was asking, so they could not understand why I was being so difficult.

Over the next several months, the tensions over the issue left us drained. I was convinced the church was wrong, but only because I thought it would hurt the poor. My wife and I quietly decided to resign.

One morning before going to work, I was praying as I watched the sun come up. I was asking God to help us say our goodbyes. Instead, he surprised me with a question: "Do you know what I think about this argument?"

I had read the Bible from cover to cover at least twenty times, and I had never trusted people who said "God told me," since I had seen that when Christians argued, emotions rose and tempers flared, especially if one person started quoting scripture to the other and claiming to have an inside word from God. Now God was asking me if I knew what he thought. I thought he was going to rebuke me for being so stubborn. As I began to think about the question, a flood of verses and stories from the Bible suddenly poured into my mind. I grabbed a pen and began writing them down.

The more I wrote, the more I realized that I had never made a careful study of what God has to say in the Bible about mercy and compassion. I had believed in Jesus since I was a child, had heard God call me to medical missions as a fourteen-year-old, had studied for fourteen years to become a doctor and a surgeon, and had read more than thirty books written by medical missionaries. I had listened to thousands of sermons from the Bible and by that time had worked as a missionary doctor in Africa for twenty years. Never once had I thought about studying the Bible systematically to see what God had to say about mercy and compassion.

Whenever I needed to make a major decision about my work and ministry, I prayed, asked God for wisdom, and then did what seemed best. My beliefs about how I carried out my service of compassion to the sick and the poor during those years was an assortment of beams and boards scavenged from all sorts of places. Some of them fit together well, but others were clearly out of place. Now that I was faced with an issue I had never encountered, I was unable to explain clearly why I was right. My "gut instinct" told me I was right, but what made my gut instinct better than that of others?

By the end of that week I had written down a rudimentary theology of compassion and mercy, based on the example and teachings of Jesus. I knew that Jesus had carried out a very significant ministry of healing during his lifetime, but I had missed how often and how much he taught his disciples about it. The Bible was filled with statements that God's desire is that his children be compassionate like he is compassionate, but I had glossed over most of it.

My rudimentary notes grew into a ten-page paper. At the end of it, I reviewed the original vision of the church, which was to serve the poor, and listed all of the miracles that God had done to accomplish the church's dream. The following week, I drove three hundred and fifty miles to the capital city and handed my paper to the church president.

The next morning the church president telephoned me and explained that he and the other church leaders needed more time to study my paper. He suggested that we meet the next morning at his office. When I showed up the next day, the church leaders were waiting. They looked tired, and I later learned that they had stayed up most of the night discussing what I had written.

The church president began in a subdued voice. "This is difficult for us, doctor, because we are pastors and church leaders. We have all gone to seminary and studied the Bible, and we teach the Bible every week to our people. You, however . . .," he paused and cleared his throat, ". . . are a doctor." He paused again, making sure I understood that I was perhaps not as knowledgeable a theologian as I thought.

"We looked up all the verses you quoted in your paper about the way we as the church should be helping the sick and using the money they give us," he continued. "We have to admit . . . " He stopped again, fiddling with his pen. "We had to admit that you are right about this."

At first I was too shocked to reply, so I just nodded and fought to keep back tears. He went on to explain that they had been looking at the hospital as a church-owned business and had forgotten what God had called them to do. As they read through my paper, they remembered how we had begun together. They were also reminded that Jesus had never healed people for profit and had never suggested to his disciples that they do so either. He acknowledged that the church was contributing nothing to the hospital, even though it belonged to them and all the pastors and their families in the church received free healthcare. They had conceived the ministry and given birth to it, but they hadn't taken care of it.

In the end, the church leaders rescinded their request that the hospital pay ten percent of its income and asked their churches to contribute to the hospital so it could do a better job of caring for the sick. From that moment on, the church took ownership of its ministry of compassion to the sick. Its contributions were never large, but they were sacrificial.

This was one of the most courageous decisions I have witnessed in my missionary career. These godly men humbled themselves before an American doctor who had never attended seminary, reversed their decision, and announced to their people that what mattered the most was not "church tradition" and not the church's need for more money to pay for its expenses, but to obey God and serve the sick *God's* way.

That conflict changed my thinking forever and forced me to question everything that I was doing as a missionary doctor. The searchlight I used to review my actions and attitudes was no longer a borrowed humanitarian flashlight or something else making the rounds, but the unchanging Word of God.

To Save A Life

Not long ago I intubated a fourteen-month-old child who was in shock, severely anemic from malaria, comatose, and gasping for air. I slipped a small, plastic tube past his tiny vocal cords and into his trachea and ventilated his lungs with pure oxygen. Malarial parasites had exploded thousands of red blood cells throughout his body and in his brain. The veins in his hands, arms and feet were all collapsed and his heart did not have enough blood to perfuse his lungs, so the oxygen flowing into his lungs was doing little to help him.

I could not get an intravenous line into the collapsed veins in his hands and arms, and the child's life continued to ebb. Every minute was critical, so I took a risk and inserted a needle deep into neck and into his internal jugular vein. We hooked up a bag of IV fluid and ran it rapidly. Within minutes the child's blood volume had increased enough to fill his heart and increase circulation to his lungs, liver, kidneys, and brain. Within minutes the child's color changed, his body warmed, and his breathing stabilized. A few minutes later, we gave him a transfusion to replace the red blood cells he had lost, administered quinine intravenously to kill the malarial parasites in his blood, and added glucose to protect him from hypoglycemia. By the next morning, the child was awake and playing on his bed.

Did we save this child's life? Most people would agree that we did, but I would argue that we did not. Using the knowledge that God had given us, we simply prolonged his life, hopefully for a long time. While nobody can know how long he will live, what is certain is that sometime within the next seventy or so years, this child will die. As all of us know, whether we want to think about it or not, none of us is going to leave this planet alive.

When our hospital first opened in south Gabon, a patient named Mahindi was the first man I operated on for a hernia. Everyone was grateful that the surgery went well and that he recovered quickly.

Mahindi lived a very long time after his operation, but despite what I did for him to prevent him from dying of a strangulated hernia, he eventually died of something else.

I once read about a man on death row who was scheduled to be executed by lethal injection for a murder he had committed. Several weeks before the execution he fell gravely ill and was rushed to a hospital so that his life could be "saved." A month later, the same people who had rushed him to the hospital carried out his execution. It would be absurd to say that his executioners had saved his life with their medical care!

It has become routine for us to consider the prolongation of life by a few years, or even of a few days, as "saving a life." This shift in emphasis is not trivial, because it has glamorized mercy and spawned a vast network of charitable NGOs (Non-Governmental Organizations) around the world, funded and staffed by an army of paid and unpaid volunteers whose goal is to better mankind. Initially, these NGO's were largely Christian, but in 1994 when the Red Cross proclaimed its "Humanitarianism Manifesto," hundreds of secular NGO's joined the parade.

A century ago we called the effort to help suffering people "being merciful." Several decades ago the terminology changed to "relief work." Now, secular multinational NGO's like the Red Cross/Red Crescent, Doctors Without Borders, Oxfam, and others have taken the spotlight and are providing the lion's share of emergency relief around the world under the banner of "saving lives." Christian organizations such as Samaritan's Purse, World Vision, World Relief and Food for the Hungry continue to play major roles, but increasingly it is the compassionate acts of celebrities and government-sanctioned secular relief organizations that dominate the headlines and captivate the world's admiration.

Over the past two decades, these organizations have been quietly resetting the world's standards for mercy. It has happened so quickly, and under such a warm glow of kindness, that many are still unaware that the ground beneath us has shifted. The world we live in today has moved beyond Christian mercy to stand on the shifting sands of secular mercy. It's critical to understand that the world's kind of mercy is not intended for the honor of God, but for the glory of Man.

Why is this important to Christians today? Christian Buckley and Ryan Dobson wrote in *Humanitarian Jesus, Social Justice and the Cross:*

> *The political and social dialogue concerning religion is largely refocusing on the idea that we can be united in love, compassion, and the betterment of mankind. Not surprisingly, the Christian church is experiencing a resurgence of the social gospel with congregations, leaders, individuals, and nonprofit groups seeking to make significant social investment in their communities and around the world. "Doing good" is a new commodity within the corporate and philanthropic worlds.* [6]

In the next chapter, we will take a closer look at "doing good" within the corporate and philanthropic worlds that Buckley and Dobson write about, and why even Christians are buying into it.

The Humanitarian Model

When my wife and I arrived in south Gabon in 1977 to start what eventually became Bongolo Hospital, we started in a three-room dispensary and a mud-brick ward with sixteen lice-infested beds. The mud walls crumbled to the touch, there were no ceilings, water, or electricity, and every morning the patients' family members had to carry water from the nearby river.

Within weeks of our arrival, there was an epidemic of measles, and all of our straw beds were soon filled with dying children. That epidemic gave way two months later to whooping cough and polio. For six months, we presided over a medical disaster. Half of the children died, and by the time we were able to fly in vaccines from Europe and vaccinate the children in every village within a one-hundred-mile radius, some five hundred children had perished.

That was thirty years ago. Today, we have buildings made from cement blocks, tiled floors, twenty-four-hour electricity, treated water, multiple medical services, and far fewer deaths. Unfortunately, we now have an entirely new crop of diseases that are lethal to both children and adults and are very difficult to subdue.

One day, one of our nurses called me to the emergency room to see a young man with a huge abdominal mass. After I examined him, I had little doubt that he had an advanced, malignant tumor of his liver. He was in severe pain and so wasted I didn't think he would live for more than a few weeks. I confirmed his diagnosis with an ultrasound. Then, as gently as I could, I gave him and his parents the bad news that I could do nothing to help him except treat his pain. His parents were too stunned to reply. The young man's mother sank to the floor and began to wail, and the boy's father struggled to speak, trying to control his emotions. In a hoarse whisper, he said to me, "But doctor, you were our last hope." I let him talk, not knowing what else to say, frustrated at my impotence.

"Everyone told us that you're the best," the boy's father cried. "That's why we came here. We've traveled for three days to get here. Isn't there *something* you can do for our son?" I sadly shook my head, wishing I could escape. The young man was now sobbing too. A small crowd of sympathetic patients from the nearby waiting area filtered into the room.

There were scabbed scratches and linear scars all over the boy's abdomen where a traditional healer had done his best to discern who in the family or the community had put a curse on the boy. The healer had taken most of the family's money in exchange for a worthless amulet that had done nothing to protect him. Now I was failing them too.

Once again, I explained to the parents that the tumor was so far advanced that it was inoperable. We had no radiation treatment or chemotherapy that would alter the tumor's course, and if I removed his liver he would die immediately. The only thing we could do for him was to give him pain medication.

By now the family had fallen silent. Their arduous and expensive journey had accomplished nothing. I took the boy's chart and began to write the dismal facts of the case. As I wrote, I explained in my best professional voice that I would hospitalize him and prescribe a narcotic for his pain. He could stay as long as he wanted, but it would cost the equivalent of twenty dollars a day.

At that, the father blinked, and his wife stood up. "Twenty dollars a day, for what?" He didn't say it, but I could read on his face what he was thinking. He finally said, "If you aren't going to help, we will go somewhere else." His wife nodded emphatically, so I gave them oral pain medication for the boy, said goodbye, and walked out of the room.

That night I did not sleep well. I had been a kind humanitarian, but I had utterly failed the patient God had sent to me. The worst part was that at that I didn't know why.

Have you ever felt that way when you tried to help someone who was suffering?

Laurie Garrett wrote in the January/February, 2007 issue of *Foreign Affairs*:

> *For the first time in history, the world is poised to spend enormous resources to conquer the diseases of the poor. Tackling the developing world's diseases has become a key feature of many nations' foreign policies over the last five years, for a variety of reasons. Some see stopping the spread of HIV, tuberculosis (TB), malaria, avian influenza, and other major killers as a moral duty. Some see it as a form of public diplomacy. And some see it as an investment in self-protection, given that microbes know no borders. Governments have been joined by a long list of private donors, topped by Bill and Melinda Gates and Warren Buffett, whose contributions to today's war on disease are mind-boggling. Thanks to their efforts, there are now billions of dollars being made available for health spending—and thousands of nongovernmental organizations (NGOs) and humanitarian groups vying to spend it.[7]*

Despite the downturn in the world economy, these initiatives continue to grow.

The seven largest humanitarian organizations in the world today are:

1. The International Committee of the Red Cross (ICRC)

2. United Nations High Commissioner for Refugees (UNHCR)

3. United Nations High Commissioner for Human Rights (UNHCHR)

4. International Federation of Red Cross and Red Crescent Societies (IFRC)

5. International Organization for Migration (IOM)

6. United Nations Children's Fund (UNICEF)

7. Department of Humanitarian Affairs (DHA)

This is only a short list of the tens of thousands of organizations that have sprung up around the globe to help the needy.

One of the highest profile organizations today is Doctors Without Borders (MSF in French). This medical humanitarian effort started in Europe in 1971 with a few volunteer doctors who were willing to go to remote and dangerous places to help the sick. Today, MSF's thousands of volunteers and paid staffers work in more than eighteen countries.

A few years ago, I was encouraged by a statement that I read on MSF's official Web site, written by a physician: "There is so little care available that the only responsible ethical position to take is action." I wondered if MSF might be a Christian organization.

As I read further I came to the second and third statements from MSF's charter:

> *MSF's decision to intervene in any country or crisis is based solely on an independent assessment of people's needs; not on political, economic, or religious interests. Members undertake to uphold their professional code of ethics and to maintain complete independence from all political, economic or religious powers.*[8]

I applauded MSF for its compassion, but I was disappointed to read in its charter that it seeks to remain a purely secular humanitarian organization and rejects religious principles as a basis for its service.

Take a moment to read below the Seven Fundamental Principles of the Red Cross:[9]

"As members of the International Red Cross and Red Crescent Movement, the American Red Cross and other national societies have a key role in upholding and abiding by the seven "Fundamental Principles":

1. Humanity: The International Red Cross and Red Crescent Movement, born of a desire to bring assistance without discrimination to the wounded on the battlefield, endeavors, in its international and national capacity, to prevent and alleviate human suffering wherever it may be found. Its purpose is to protect life and health and to ensure respect for the human being. It promotes mutual understanding, friendship, cooperation and lasting peace amongst all peoples.

2. Impartiality: It makes no discrimination as to nationality, race, religious beliefs, class or political opinions. It endeavors to relieve the suffering of individuals, being guided solely by their needs, and to give priority to the most urgent cases of distress.

3. Neutrality: In order to continue to enjoy the confidence of all, the Movement may not take sides in hostilities or engage at any time in controversies of a political, racial, religious or ideological nature.

4. Independence: The Movement is independent. The National Societies, while auxiliaries in the humanitarian services of their governments and subject to the laws of their respective countries, must always maintain their autonomy so that they may be able at all times to act in accordance with the principles of the Movement.

5. Voluntary service: It is a voluntary relief movement not prompted in any manner by desire for gain.

6. Unity: There can be only one Red Cross or Red Crescent Society in any one country. It must be open to all. It must carry on its humanitarian work throughout its territory.

7. Universality: The International Red Cross and Red Crescent Movement, in which all Societies have equal status and share equal responsibilities and duties in helping each other, is worldwide.

These are laudable principles that parallel in some ways the teachings and example of Jesus Christ. Most of them might even be shared by some of the great religions of the world. However, they differ in three very important ways from what Christ taught:

1. Their concern for people ends at the grave.
2. They do not acknowledge God's influence on their thinking and have no place for him in their work.
3. They present Man as the only true deliverer in a tragically flawed world.

These humanitarian principles appear to flow from two contradictory sources: Biblical Christianity and a secular belief system that holds that nothing exists in the universe apart from the material world—including God himself. This belief system is now so powerful that to challenge it is to risk one's professional standing and employment. It holds that if something cannot be scientifically measured or experienced by one or more of our five senses, it cannot be part of the "material," or real world. The marriage of the biblical teaching of mercy with the secular humanitarian system is only possible because secular humanitarianism has swallowed the other and rephrased it in its own terms.

The majority of medical professionals who have been educated in the world's secular universities accept the Red Cross's seven humanitarian principles listed at the beginning of this discussion, as well as the MSF physician's statement that "There is so little care available that the only responsible ethical position to take is action."

Secular humanism is far removed from the MSF physician's statement. How does helping the weak survive advance the process of natural selection? How do mercy and compassion for the helpless move Man to a higher, more intelligent and stronger species? Aren't humanitarians actually impeding human progress?

If the reasons for helping the weak are the ethical ones pulled out of thin air by popular vote, then why should Christians want to embrace them? It's safe to say that the modern humanitarianism movement is not being driven by the atheistic ideology its supporters claim to follow, but by a pure, feel-good emotionalism that is borrowed from the West's Christian heritage.

Christians who embrace the humanitarian model of compassion and mercy have not chosen a more reasonable or workable model, but one that contradicts both itself and faith in a loving God.

Atheistic Western Medicine

I graduated from the University of Pittsburgh as a medical doctor in 1973. During my years in the university, I was told that my education was based on the great pillar of learning called the scientific method, which is still defined today as "a method of investigation involving observation and theory to test scientific hypotheses"[10] Scientific studies conducted on the basis of this principle have regularly discovered new and better ways to treat injury and disease. This effectiveness in discerning things as they really are explains why the scientific method has become the guiding light of modern Western research and medicine. At the same time, belief in God's revelation in the Bible about the origin of life and of human beings, the existence of the spiritual world, the Fall of Man, and the disastrous effect of sin on the human race and in history has been replaced by an outlook that leaves no room for God.

Interestingly enough, modern science, as we know it, was not discovered by the Greeks, the Chinese, or by the Arabs, but by eminent Christian scientists in Western Europe during the seventeenth century. Rodney Stark pointed out in his book, *For the Glory of God, How Monotheism Led to Reformations, Science, With-Hunts, and the End of Slavery* that the evidence that modern science emerged in the seventeenth century in Western Europe is indisputable. He stated, "Christianity depicted God as a rational, responsive, dependable, and omnipotent being and the universe as his personal creation...

Christians developed science because they believed it could be done, and should be done."[11]

As a medical student I studied human anatomy and physiology in exhaustive detail. The more I learned, the more my amazement grew at how "fearfully and wonderfully" the human body was made.

During my third year of medical school, I took a three-month clinical rotation in obstetrics and gynecology. One day, several of us watched a gynecologist suction a live fetus out of a woman's uterus. The suction device tore the fetus into pieces and dumped its parts into a clear plastic container near our feet. The professor performing the operation calmly explained that when performed legally, such procedures were good for society. Having a highly-trained professional rid a woman of her unwanted fetus in a sterile operating room provided a clean solution to one of society's more unpleasant social problems. He admitted that the mother's life was not at risk, but that it was justified because she did not want the child. This had nothing to do with *science*. Nevertheless, the idea that abortions are good for society remains one of the tenets of atheistic Western medicine.

At a major surgical conference in 2007 in New Orleans, I was astonished to hear a distinguished lecturer from Brazil claim that when more abortions were performed in Brazil, fewer homicides occurred. He postulated that unwanted children were somehow related to homicides, so killing them in their mothers' wombs before birth was good for society. I came close to standing up to question his study, but at that point in the meeting he was given an award for his distinguished achievements in medicine.

What few in the audience seemed to understand was that this man's claim ran counter to scientific principles. The scientific method cannot argue that we who are living today are evolutionarily superior to fetuses. We were simply born first, allowed by our parents to live, and have seized for ourselves the power of life and death over our fetuses for our personal convenience.

to live, and have seized for ourselves the power of life and death over our fetuses for our personal convenience.

In the three decades following the legalization of abortion in the United States, the number of aborted children swelled to more than 1 million a year. Between 1973 and 2008, more than fifty *million* abortions were carried out in the United States.[12] In contrast to what the eminent Brazilian surgeon claimed to have discovered in his country, since abortions became legal in the United States in 1973, the incidence of child abuse and homicide has skyrocketed, with no end in sight.

How many possible future mathematicians, gifted scientists, compassionate doctors, wise teachers, courageous soldiers, or even Nobel Prize winners over the years have been carried out of university hospitals in trash bags to be incinerated in large ovens? If atheistic Western medicine is neither logical nor morally right, why are so many professional Christians apparently embracing it without questions?

During my later clinical rotations in medical school, I learned another important truth: it is professionally unacceptable for a doctor to talk to a dying person about God. The reasons for this were varied, but mainly centered on two issues: 1) it seems unfair, and therefore immoral, and 2) it is unscientific, since God can neither be examined nor proven by science.

To my knowledge, no one has yet been able to study God using the scientific method. It would therefore seem reasonable to conclude that God's existence can't be proved or disproved by this method. In today's world, however, you would be considered wrong to believe that. Why? Because if God cannot be measured by the scientific method, he only exists in people's imaginations. We can't prove the existence of the human mind apart from the brain either, but few of us are foolish enough to believe that it doesn't exist.

There is only one place where modern science concedes God's usefulness, and that is when a patient's belief in God appears to help him emotionally. This reduces faith to a useful crutch, a calming fantasy for the dying. Since the emotionally weak are the only ones who need it, faith in God represents no threat to atheistic Western medicine.

By the end of medical school, I understood perfectly that if I wanted to be considered a "man of science." I would have to toe the party line. I really did want to be an exceptional doctor, so for a while I took care not to talk to any of my patients about God. With very little effort, I got used to keeping my religious life and beliefs private and separate from my medical practice. I could be a Christian at home and an atheist at work.

In the end, though, it was the intellectual dishonesty and spiritual poverty of atheistic Western medicine that drove me back to the model of Jesus. Atheistic Western medicine left me without a rational argument for compassion. It encouraged instead selfishness and cruelty.

Theistic Western medicine has always welcomed God's partnership, but over the past few decades it has been taken hostage by atheists. It no longer provides answers for the sick and dying, and fails to protect those whom society deems burdensome. As a consistent, moral guide for Christians wanting to serve the sick with compassion, it fails.

Chapter 3
TROJAN HORSES

Hezekiah received the Babylonian envoys and showed them every-thing in his treasure-houses—the silver, the gold, the spices, and the aromatic oils. He also took them to see his armory and showed them everything in his royal treasuries! There was nothing in his palace or kingdom that Hezekiah did not show them.

2 Kings 20:13

T he story about the Trojan Horse was written nearly two thousand years ago by Homer in the Iliad. No one knows if the story is based on fact or fiction, but it is one of the most famous stories in Western literature.

The story took place during a long war between the Greeks and the Trojans. Despite a ten-year siege that included many fierce battles, the Greeks were unable to conquer the city of Troy. One morning when the sun came up, the people of Troy were surprised to find that the Greek army had apparently sailed away, leaving an enor-mous wooden horse outside the city's main gate. The Trojans learned from a deserter that the Greeks had sailed away in defeat and left the wooden horse as an offering to their gods. After confirming that the Greek fleet was gone, the people broke down the front gate and dragged the wooden horse inside. That night the Greek army silently returned. As the people of Troy celebrated their victory, thirty select warriors hidden inside the wooden horse slipped out and opened all the city gates. Troy was conquered and its people were taken into slavery. Because of this story, a "Trojan Horse" has come to mean any gift that is invited into one's home or heart that turns out to be a destroying enemy. In the computer world, it refers to "malware," a term which describes "a seemingly useful computer program that contains concealed instructions which when activated, perform an illicit or malicious action (as destroying data files)."[13]

Healthcare as Business

In Chapter 2 I told the story of how for a time the leaders of the church that owned the hospital where I worked thought it would be a blessing to turn it into a business. The model of "healthcare-as-business" is enormously appealing to church-run hospitals in the developing world, especially in Africa. Healthcare-as-business is not unchristian, so what happens when it is practiced in the name of the Church?

In 2006, I visited one such hospital in Africa. On Sunday morning I sat in a lovely little church on the hospital's campus with about one hundred hospital employees and their families. The singing was beautiful, and the sound of our singing drifted across the campus and into the open windows of the wards. It probably even wafted to the front door of the recently modernized emergency department, a place where men, women and children were regularly carried in bleeding, crying in pain from obstructed labor or hemorrhaging from traumatic motor vehicle injuries. The songs we sang were a combination of the classic hymns of the Christian faith and choruses written in the local language. I was uplifted and inspired, and rejoiced that this hospital appeared to be staffed by people who loved Jesus Christ.

The next day I visited the emergency department and learned that when patients arrived there, they were gently laid on the clean sheets of modern gurneys and attended to by nurses dressed in crisp, white uniforms. The nurses' first mission, after they took care of the usual medical preliminaries, was to establish how much it would cost the patient to be treated. If the family had the resources to pay immediately for the patient's care, then normal emergency services would be immediately and professionally provided. If, however, the patient did not have enough to pay a major proportion of the anticipated hospital costs up front and in cash, the nurses had clear instructions to stop all services until the money was paid. If the family said they could not pay, they were told to call a taxi to take their loved one elsewhere. This policy was carried out in all of the hospital's departments.

One night during my visit, a very young woman was brought to the maternity ward in obstructed labor. It was her first baby and her pelvis was too small for the baby's head to pass through the birth canal. She had been in labor for more than twenty-four hours and was dehydrated, exhausted from the effort, and bleeding. She needed an emergency blood transfusion and a C-section. Unfortunately, her family had only enough money to pay for a single bag of IV fluid. The midwives caring for the girl turned the IV down to a few drops a minute and walked away. Despite the family's pleas for mercy, they refused to do anything more until the family paid the full cost of the C-section. The family replied that they did not have the money and were doing their best to collect it from relatives both near and far.

The next morning a surgical colleague of mine discovered the young woman lying unconscious in a pool of blood and in severe shock. Stunned by what he found, he paid the woman's bill, ordered intravenous fluids and a blood transfusion, and rushed her to the operating room for an emergency C-section. He delivered a live but severely depressed baby. The mother died a few hours later from irreversible shock, and several hours later the baby died as well. The hospital blamed the family for failing to come up with the money in time.

When my friend asked the hospital officials how they could be so heartless, they replied that they had no choice. If they treated such people without demanding payment in advance, the hospital would not have enough money to pay for medications or pay its employees. If the employees weren't paid they would quit, and then the hospital would have to close. This was the hospital's policy by necessity, and it was backed by the well-known denomination that owned the hospital. I later learned that the denomination routinely accessed the hospital's bank account when it needed funds, further limiting the hospital's ability to care for the poor.

In the months that followed, my colleague witnessed even worse things, including patients who were allowed to bleed to death in the emergency room while the nurses sat at their desk and chatted. Not surprisingly, the attitude of the predominantly Muslim community served by this hospital was one of anger and despair.

This is not an isolated case. In fact, many of Africa's once great Christian hospitals have been encouraged to embrace the "medicine-as-business" model by the denominations that created them so they will be "self-sustaining." These hospitals continue to call their medical services "ministries of the church." These hospitals have succeeded in saving themselves and helping their denominational leaders meet their budgets, but at the cost of sacrificing the poor. Is this what Jesus taught his followers to do?

When the people of Israel adopted a similar attitude towards the poor, God spoke to them through the prophet Isaiah and gave them a way out:

Stop bringing meaningless offerings! Your incense is detestable to me. New Moons, Sabbaths and convocations—I cannot bear your evil assemblies . . . my soul hates [them]. When you spread out your hands in prayer, I will hide my eyes from you; even if you offer many prayers, I will not listen. Your hands are full of blood; wash and make yourselves clean. Take your evil deeds out of my sight! Stop doing wrong, learn to do right! Seek justice, encourage the oppressed. Defend the cause of the fatherless, plead the cause of the widow. (Isaiah 1:13-17)

It is one thing to use the fees that patients pay for their healthcare services to provide them with compassionate medical services and insure that there are resources on hand for urgent patient care. It is quite another matter to take those same fees and use them to pay pastors, administrators, or church budgets. And where in all of this is faith, that priceless commodity without which it is impossible to please God? When Jesus said to his disciples in Matthew 7:7-8, "Keep on asking and you will receive what you ask for. Keep on seeking, and you will find. Keep on knocking, and the door will be opened to you. For everyone who asks, receives. Everyone who seeks, finds. And to everyone who knocks, the door will be opened" was he kidding?

The healthcare-as-business model of a church-based compassion ministry is not supported by any teaching found in the Bible. What Jesus taught and modeled was the exact opposite. In Matthew 10:8 he said to his disciples, "Heal the sick, raise the dead, cure those with leprosy, and cast out demons. *Give as freely as you have received!*" (*emphasis* mine). Nowhere did he even suggest to his followers that they create institutions in his name to treat the wealthy and turn away the poor!

Compassion for the poor was taught throughout the Old Testament as a sign of godliness. "Whoever gives to the poor will lack nothing, but those who close their eyes to poverty will be cursed" (Proverbs 28:27). "The godly care about the rights of the poor; the wicked don't care at all" (Proverbs 29:7).

Like a Trojan horse, the attractive idea that churches can and should profit from the sick for whatever reason looks and sounds good, but sows the seeds of hypocrisy and cruelty.

The Social Gospel

A second Trojan horse for today's Christian is the newly resurgent theological teaching that came to be known in the early 1900s as "the Social Gospel." John Stott summarized the origins and reasons for the movement in his book *Issues Facing Christians Today*:

> *It's most popular spokesman was Walter Rauschenbush, who was Professor of Church History at Rochester Seminary, New York, from 1897 to 1917. . . . He . . . contrasted 'the old evangel of the saved soul' with 'the new evangel of the Kingdom of God.' 'It is not a matter of getting individuals into heaven,' he wrote, 'but of transforming the life on earth into the harmony of heaven.'* [14]

Influential ministers in England and the United States raised the popularity of the social gospel by proposing that Darwinism could be applied to society as well as to biology. The theology of salvation through repentance and faith in Christ alone was hijacked for the broader need of society in general to be transformed, ushering in the Millennium as described in Revelation, chapter 20. Very few Christians today know this story.

In his introduction to *The Social Gospel in America,* published in 1966, Robert Handy summarized the movement as follows:

> *A complex and dynamic movement in history, the social gospel was variously expressed by its several generations of leaders, yet its main emphases can be rather briefly stated. These include a conviction that the social principles of the historical Jesus could serve as reliable guides for both individual and social life in any age. Central to his teachings, so these liberal social Christians*

believed, was a stress on the imminence of God, the goodness and worth of man, and the coming kingdom of God on earth. Indeed, they affirmed, at the very heart of his gospel was the message of the kingdom, which they interpreted as a possibility within history. Though the church had long ago lost the true key to the kingdom, now that key had been recovered. The spokesmen for the social gospel expected that, through the efforts of men of good will, the kingdom of God would soon become a reality, bringing with it social harmony and the elimination of the worst of social injustices. . . . Through determined moral effort, men could hasten the day of the coming of the empire of law and love, the kingdom of God.[15]

This powerful movement had the unfortunate effect of downplaying the importance of the verbal proclamation of the gospel. In North America and on foreign fields around the world—where evangelism had previously been a major objective—the emphasis gradually shifted towards the sacrificial, compassionate, *professional* ministry to the sick and the poor, without the verbal gospel.

The shift from preaching the gospel to simply *exemplifying* the gospel through works of compassion did not go unnoticed. Many Christian leaders denounced the movement, including an evangelist named Paul Rader. The following statement is taken from his 1912-1913 President's Report to the Annual Meeting of his church, the Christian and Missionary Alliance:

The Gospel of Jesus Christ does not have to play second fiddle to any hospital, school or civilizing scheme. The Gospel is God's great pioneer. It opens the path, it plows the furrows, it plants the seed. Then the hospitals, schools and civilizing, uplifting schemes come on behind. Look what the enemy has done. He has taken this perfectly good, four-wheeled wagon of hospitals, schools, civilization, and science, and fastened them successfully before the great gospel horse.

Some who served in Christian hospitals welcomed this teaching because it eliminated the tension between healing the sick and preaching to them. Now overworked professionals and medical missionaries could concentrate on what they were trained to do, which was to practice Western medicine. Within a few years, pastors and evangelists were given lower ranking than administrators, accountants, and medical professionals. They were invited to pray for patients and talk to them individually, but only as long as they did not interfere with what the doctors, nurses, and accountants felt was appropriate.

In 1921, Mennonite historian John Horsch wrote in *Modern Religious Liberalism*,

> *. . . the new view of missions includes more than mere mutual interpretation of religion. Its burden is the social gospel. Instead of working for the salvation of individuals by faith in our Lord Jesus Christ, it undertakes to save society by socialization and reforms of various descriptions.*[16]

Within a few decades, the hospitals of the mainline Protestant denominations in Europe and North America ceased to verbally proclaim Christ to the sick. By the 1950s, most Protestant hospitals in North American had become secular in everything but name.

By 1920, in hundreds of Christian hospitals and clinics around the world, the damage had been done. Worse yet, the pendulum had swung so far in the direction of humanistic efforts to save the world that several decades later, when there was a strong movement to return to an emphasis on the verbal preaching of the gospel, churches reversed course and actively *opposed* compassionate ministries in the Protestant church for nearly a century.

In their book *When Helping Hurts,* Steve Corbett and Brian
Fikkert trace the decline of the evangelical protestant church's ministry to the poor in the United States to an overreaction to the social
gospel. They wrote:

> *Evangelicals interpreted the rising social gospel movement,*
> *which seemed to equate all humanitarian efforts with bringing*
> *in Christ's kingdom, as part of the overall theological drift of*
> *the nation. As evangelicals tried to distance themselves from the*
> *social gospel movement, they ended up in large-scale retreat*
> *from the front lines of poverty alleviation. This shift away from*
> *the poor was so dramatic that church historians refer to the*
> *1900-1930's as the "Great Reversal" in the evangelical church's*
> *approach to social problems.*[17]

This near abandonment of service to the poor by American
evangelicals and what Corbett and Fikkert describe as "lacking
appreciation of the comprehensive implications of the kingdom of
God" had consequences that would shock the world during the civil
war in Rwanda when the majority racial tribe in the country did its
best to exterminate its rival tribe. Corbett and Fikkert wrote:

> *The consequences of this truncated gospel have been devastat-*
> *ing in the Majority World in general and in Africa in particular.*
> *There is perhaps no better example of this than Rwanda. Despite*
> *the fact that 80 percent of Rwandans claimed to be Christians,*
> *a bloody civil war erupted in 1994 in which the Hutu majority*
> *conducted a brutal genocide against the Tutsi minority and Hutu*
> *moderates. Over a three-month period, an estimated 800,000*
> *people were slaughtered, the vast majority of them Tutsis.*[18]

Engle and Dyrness explained in their book about the Rwandan
massacre, *Where Have We Gone Wrong?* that before the massacre the
Rwandan church "was silent on such critical life-and-death issues as
the dignity and worth of each person made in the image of God."[19]

In his book, *Everything Must Change*, Brian McLaren described a meeting of fifty-five Rwandan pastors that took place several years after the massacre of 1994. Most were from the Hutu and Tutsi tribes. The pastor leading the meeting asked his colleagues if any of them had ever heard "even one sermon telling Tutsi people to love and reconcile with Hutu people, or Hutu people to love and reconcile with Tutsi."[20] He wrote that two Anglican priests raised their hands and admitted that they had only preached those sermons *after* the massacre.

Later in his book McLaren quoted the complaint of a young healthcare worker from Rwanda about his church:

> It has specialized in dealing with "spiritual needs" to the exclusion of physical and social needs. It has specialized in people's destination in the afterlife but has failed to address significant social injustices in this life. It has focused on "me" and "my soul" and "my spiritual life" and "my eternal destiny," but it has failed to address the dominant societal and global realities of their lifetime: systemic injustice, systemic poverty, systemic ecological crisis, systemic dysfunctions of many kinds.[21]

McLaren's diagnosis was that the message we call "the gospel" should do better than this. It should be "a vibrant form of Christian faith that is holistic, integral, and balanced—one that offers good news for both the living and the dying, that speaks of God's grace at work both in this life and the life to come, that speaks to individuals and to societies and to the planet as a whole."[22]

This is a statement with which I can wholeheartedly agree, but McLaren then pushed the pendulum forcefully back in the direction of the old social gospel. Looking at the violence, confusion, pollution, and injustice in the world, he asked what should be done about the mess we're in and gave this answer:

Jesus came to become Savior of the world, meaning he came to save the earth and all it contains from its ongoing destruction because of human evil. Through his life and teaching, through his suffering, death, and resurrection, he inserted into human a seed of grace, truth, and hope that can never be defeated. This seed will, against all opposition and odds, prevail over the evil and injustice of humanity and lead to the world's ongoing transforming into the world God dreams of. All who find in Jesus God's hope and truth discover the privilege of participating in his ongoing work of personal and global transformation and liberation from evil and injustice. As part of his transforming community, they experience liberation from the fear of death and condemnation. This is not something they earn or achieve, but rather a free gift they receive as an expression of God's grace and love. [23]*

A chapter later McLaren shoved the pendulum even more forcefully in the direction of the old social gospel: "The Bible . . . is the story of the partnership between God and humanity to save and transform all of human society and avert global self-destruction." [24]

Any hope one might have had that McLaren had based his doctrine of compassionate action to save the world on the teachings and model of Jesus faded with these words:

Fundamentalist religious movements . . . take words spoken five hundred or fourteen hundred or two thousand years ago and apply them sharia-*style, as if they were intended to serve as today's annotated legal code, today's constitution, today's how-to manual. They underestimate how the original words and teach-ings were situated—how deeply their sacred texts were rooted in gritty contemporary problems and human contexts; instead, they see their sacred texts as timeless, placeless utterances coming from an arid, Platonic plane of universal abstractions. . . . This naiveté is so pervasive and so accepted that one can hardly blame people for being taken in by it.*[25]

McLaren based his call to return to the social gospel not on the Bible, but on his own ability to discern between "naiveté" and truth.

The repercussions of the social gospel have been shaking Christendom for nearly one hundred years, in large part because well-meaning Christians and their leaders reacted too vigorously to the social gospel that was embraced in 1910. When God's people finally realized their mistake, they reacted so forcefully in the opposite direction that they set the pendulum swinging again.

One of the purposes of this book is to *stop* this theological pendulum from swinging back and forth. Christians in this age need to set their beliefs on the solid rock of Jesus Christ and his teachings, and not just on the teachings about mercy and compassion they prefer!

We need to realize that we live in a world which prides itself on bringing organizations and diverse religious groups together under common umbrellas to fight problems like AIDS, poverty, hunger, and other social ills. But to proclaim even *gently* that "There is salvation in no one else! God has given no other name under heaven by which we must be saved!" (Acts 4:12) is to invoke a firestorm of criticism. The strong temptation for Christians involved in mercy and compassionate ministries today is to remain silent for the sake of harmony.

In Matthew 10:34, Jesus warned his disciples about this very problem: "Don't imagine that I came to bring peace to the earth! I came not to bring peace, but a sword!" If our highest aspirations are to make people happy, offend no one, and ignore spiritual lostness, we will be serving someone other than Jesus.

In John 17:18, Jesus prayed for his disciples in the upper room. He said, "Just as you sent me into the world I am sending them into the world." After his death and resurrection, he announced to his disciples, *"As the Father has sent me, so I am sending you"* (John 20:21, *emphasis* mine). With these two statements he drew a parallel between his mission and ours.

Commenting on these two verses, John Stott wrote in *Christian Mission*:

> *Jesus did more than draw a vague parallel between his mission and ours. Deliberately and precisely he made his mission the model of ours, when he said, "as the Father sent me, so I send you" [emphasis mine]. Therefore our understanding of the church's mission must be deduced from our understanding of the Son's.*[26]

The answer to stopping the swinging of the pendulum of mercy and compassion is so simple that some Christians working in the field miss it entirely: *Jesus is our model and the Bible is our guide.* It is not what is most popular or what seems to work the best that counts, but what Jesus taught and lived. This is what must be our guiding light. After all, God is the father of mercy, so if we are to act mercifully in his name and with his blessing, we must do it his way.

In Jeremiah 2:8, God said to his people, "Those who taught my word ignored me." In Psalm 50:16 God says, "Why bother reciting my decrees and pretending to obey my covenant? For you refuse my discipline and treat my words like trash".

Whose teachings and decrees are we following? Have we invited Trojan horses into our hearts, our churches and our seminaries? Are we ignoring God so we can please men? Franklin Graham stated in an interview that he gave in the book *Humanitarian Jesus*, "I'm afraid to say that many churches today are compromising their spending, and even their preaching to attract the world's attention."[27]

How important is this issue? It turns out to be immensely important, because unless we choose God's way we will repeat the mistake the people of Troy made. After fiercely resisting the Trojans for ten years, during a moment of foolish celebration they lost everything and were enslaved by their enemies.

Chapter 4

CLOSE ENCOUNTERS

When he saw the man . . .
Luke 10:33

I n the January/February 2007 edition of *Foreign Affairs*, Laurie Garette wrote:

Perched along the verdant hillsides of South Africa's KwaZulu-Natal Province are tin-roofed mud-and-wood houses, so minimal that they almost seem to shiver in the winter winds. An observant eye will spot bits of carved stone laying flat among the weeds a few steps from the round houses, under which lay the deceased. The stones are visible evidence of a terrifying death toll, as this Zulu region may well have the highest HIV prevalence rate in the world.

At the top of one hill in the Vulindlela area resides Chief Inkosi Zondi. A quiet man in his early 40s, Zondi shakes his head over the AIDS horror. "We can say there are 40,000 people in my 18 subdistricts," he says. "Ten thousand have died. So about 25 percent of the population has died." In this rugged area, only about ten percent of the adults have formal employment, and few young people have much hope of a reasonable future. Funerals are the most commonplace form of social gathering. Law and order are unraveling, despite Chief Zondi's best efforts, because the police and the soldiers are also dying of AIDS.[28]

There are more than six billion people in the world, and at any given time a significant portion of them are sick, injured, or dying. An estimated one billion live on less than one dollar a day, twenty-five thousand die each day from starvation and poverty, and one hundred million are homeless. God only knows how many are living like the survivors in KwaZulu-Natal. With so many in need, how are we supposed to decide which ones to help? If we help the hungry in Africa but not those in central Asia, what will happen to those we ignore? If we feed the hungry but ignore the sick, how have we made a difference? If we expend all our strength and resources to stop the horror of AIDS in KwaZulu-Natal Province but do nothing to help the 1.6 million children and adults in Africa who die each year of malaria, have we done well? Except for a few people like Bill and Linda Gates, we as individuals do not have either the time or the resources to help everyone who needs help. So how do we choose?

An Ancient Story

A story is told about a man in ancient times who left his home early one morning and set out on foot with his donkey loaded with wares for a city several days away. He had not gone far when bandits jumped him, beat him senseless, and stole everything he had, including most of his clothes.

He lay alongside the road for hours before another traveler came along and noticed him. By that time he was probably conscious but too weak to stand or walk. The passerby was a Jewish priest who should have stopped to help, but for some reason, turned away and kept going.

What went through his mind? He surely saw that the man was suffering, but apparently he did not grieve for him. Was he afraid of being attacked by the same bandits? Did he think God was judging the injured man for his sin and it wasn't his business to interfere?

The storyteller did not say. He only stated that this religious leader who knew better, turned and walked away.

A little while later another traveler walked down the same road and saw the injured man. He, too, was a religious leader, from the Jewish tribe of Levi. He should have helped the man but kept on walking.

What was he thinking? Maybe he thought the injured man was foolish for setting out alone so early in the morning. Why should he take responsibility for another's man's stupidity? We will never know, but his failure to respond with effective action revealed a moral flaw that every listener to the story recognized.

Shortly after the second man left, a third traveler walked into view. This man was from a race that the other three characters in the story despised. He was a Samaritan, half Jewish and half Assyrian. Everyone listening expected to hear that he, too, walked on by. But as soon as he saw the injured man, he stopped and began to help him. He grieved for him, did not condemn him, and took urgent, effective action. He washed the injured man's wounds and covered them with strips of cloth, perhaps torn from his own clothing. Then he lifted the injured man onto his donkey and took him to the nearest hotel. At the hotel he paid for a room—not just for the night but for as long as the man would need it.

The storyteller then asked his listeners which one of the three travelers loved his neighbor? They answered that the Samaritan loved his neighbor. The storyteller was Jesus, and he said to his listeners, "Go and do the same." (Luke 10:37)

With this brief story, Jesus taught his followers how he wanted them to respond to the injured and suffering people they encountered. Jesus was saying to all of his followers that *we are to help those who are suffering that we encounter and not turn away from them!*

A Freeway Encounter

When I was a surgery resident in Los Angeles, I drove into the downtown area from my home in the suburbs at 5:30 each weekday morning. One morning as I flew around a long curve on the three-lane freeway at sixty-five miles per hour, I saw an injured man lying in the center lane. His motorcycle was thirty yards down the road on the shoulder. Several cars in front of me swerved around him on both sides at speeds of fifty to sixty miles per hour.

As a surgeon in training, I had considerable experience treating trauma victims. I knew that if I did not stop to protect him, it would not be long before someone ran him over. Without thinking, I slammed on my brakes and stopped my compact car ten feet in front of the injured man. Then I turned on the car's flashers, jumped from my car and ran to help. The man was unconscious, breathing noisily and irregularly, but still alive. He had a good pulse and no obvious bleeding, so I stabilized his neck and as I had been trained, made sure his airway was fully open. For the next five minutes, hundreds of cars whizzed by on both sides as I held the man's head and neck. If I let go of him while he was unconscious, he could strangle and die, or his head might flop to one side and worsen a possible spinal cord injury. I couldn't move until someone else stopped to help, and there was nothing more I could do except pray that God would give someone driving by the courage to stop and help us.

A few minutes later a car stopped in the lane next to me, and the driver got out, called 911 on his cell phone, and began directing traffic. Twenty minutes later, an ambulance showed up and took over from me. I later learned that the injured man recovered, though he had a concussion and multiple fractures.

I never got the name of the man who stopped to direct traffic and called for help, but I thank God for him. Both of us risked our lives, neither of us profited financially, and nobody thanked us, although one of the EMTs criticized me sharply for having the nerve to touch the injured man before he arrived! According to what Jesus taught in his story of the Good Samaritan, of all the people who encountered the injured man on the freeway that day, we were the ones who loved him.

In his book *The Samaritan Way,* David W. Crocker wrote:

I am intrigued by these two men who passed up their chance to be a hero and hurried on their way. Did they wonder whether they did the right thing in passing by without so much as lifting a finger to help, or were they so programmed not to defile themselves that they hardly gave it a thought? Did their guts tighten the next time they prayed for the downtrodden? Did they tell their wives what happened when they got home that night, or were they too ashamed to mention it? Did they lie awake at night unable to close their eyes, because every time they did images of a beaten, bloody man tormented them? Were they reminded of their failure every time thereafter they traveled the Jerusalem-Jericho Turnpike? Did they use this situation as a case study in teaching Jewish young men the importance of discipline—not to give in to questionable needs where there is a chance of ceremonial defilement? How did these two deal with their part in the story.[29]

What was the difference between the Samaritan and the two religious leaders who turned away? Crocker sums it up in two brief sentences: "Because of his compassion, the Samaritan asked not, 'What will happen to me if I stop?' which is what the Priest and Levite probably asked themselves, but 'What will happen to this man *if I do not stop?*'"[30]

During the three years of his ministry, Jesus spent about half of his time healing the sick. The rest of the time he preached.

Jesus traveled to wherever the Spirit of God directed him. Like the Samaritan in the story, Jesus helped those he *encountered*, perhaps motivated by the question, "What will happen if I do not stop and help them?"

At times, the crowds must have exhausted him. There were days when all he did from morning until night was touch people and heal them. When one person was cured, another took his place. Some days he didn't even have time to eat. But not once in the accounts written by Matthew, Mark, Luke, and John do we read that Jesus turned away from someone who asked for help. He always helped, although once when a woman from Phoenicia demanded him to heal her daughter, he tested her to see how much she believed in him. When she gave an answer that demonstrated great faith, he healed her daughter on the spot.

After the death and resurrection of Jesus, his disciples followed this same pattern *of helping those they encountered*. They went where the Spirit of God directed them, healed those they encountered who needed help, and told them about Jesus the Messiah and the forgiveness from sin that he offered. They did exactly what Jesus showed them to do, and God honored and blessed them for it.

Whether we care to acknowledge it or not, the four gospels document that Jesus' four predominant activities were prayer, healing, preaching, and delivering people from oppression by evil spirits. The two things that he did the most were prayer and preaching but the human suffering that he encountered drew him irresistibly to help the sick and those oppressed by evil spirits.

Though preaching the gospel was Jesus' priority, he did not ignore the sick in the audience. If a person came and asked him for help, he healed him, even if it got him into trouble with the Jewish leaders. He followed the same pattern when he provided food for the thousands of hungry people who walked far from their homes to hear his teaching.

It would be a mistake to conclude that Jesus' various ministries were not integrally related. Again and again he told the people he helped, "Your *faith* has made you well." (Matthew 9:29).

Are Today's Encounters Random?

When I applied to medical school, I didn't know anyone who had the pull to help me get accepted over all the other candidates, other than God, of course! I had worked very hard in college to get good grades and done everything in my power to qualify, but because there were so many other qualified candidates, my chances of getting into medical school were probably less than one in ten. Somehow my application to medical school landed on the desk of Dr. William B. Kiesewetter, the Chief of Pediatric Surgery at Children's Hospital in Pittsburgh.

When I was fourteen years old, I witnessed the death of a man on the side of the road in Cambodia. My father and I tried to help him, but we had neither the training or the resources. Seeing that we could do nothing more, my father tried to share the gospel with him in Cambodian, but the injured man was a Buddhist. After a moment he asked my father to stop, rejecting his only hope for eternal life. From then on, I began to ask God to allow me to become a missionary doctor who could help the injured and dying and give them the opportunity to hear and understand the good news of Jesus *before* it was too late. It was not by chance that I arrived that day on the scene of that accident, but God's divine appointment.

When I filled out my application to medical schools, that story was part of my answer to the question, "Why do you want to become a doctor?" So I was thrilled when in April, 1969, Dr. Kiesewetter's secretary called me and asked me to come for an interview in his office at the University of Pittsburgh School of Medicine.

Once I got over my excitement, I was terrified! What kind of a man was he? What would he say about my dream of becoming a Christian missionary doctor? I knew that he had the power to end my dream.

Almost from the outset of my interview, Dr. Kiesewetter challenged me to explain why I wanted to become a missionary doctor and what I would do if I became one. I talked and sweated for forty-five minutes as this great professor of pediatric surgery looked at me over the top of his reading glasses and listened impassively. Then, with a twinkle in his eye and a smile, he told me he was a follower of Jesus! Not only that, but he thought my dream to become a medical missionary was wonderful. With a stroke of his pen and a few phone calls, I was in.

Several months later, Dr. Kiesewetter and his wife invited me to live with them in their beautiful home in Pittsburgh. Later they helped me apply for a grant from the Pennsylvania Medical Missions Society that eventually paid all my tuition for the next four years. When I graduated, I was one of the few students in my class to leave without any debts. I knew without a shadow of a doubt that God had arranged my encounter with Dr. Kiesewetter.

In 2004 I traveled to Cambodia for the first time in thirty-eight years. During my visit, God arranged another remarkable encounter.

Between 1949 and 1964, our family had lived in Kratie, Cambodia. The country was and still is overwhelmingly Buddhist. After Cambodia won its independence from the French, the government paid lip service to religious freedom but in fact did everything it could to stymie the work of Christian missionaries. Soon after my parents arrived in Kratie, the governor called my father into his office and told him he could not preach or start a church. He drew a circle with his finger around our town on a map and stated that outside that circle my parents could preach and establish a church, but not inside.

The nearest village outside of that circle was the tiny village of Kabal Chua, twelve kilometers away. So that's where my parents planted a church.

After ten years, the church had grown to about forty adult believers. Eventually a Cambodian pastor named Kru On was assigned by the Evangelical Church of Cambodia to lead the church, freeing my parents up to preach in many other villages in the province. My father and Kru On became fast friends. Kru On married and fathered five children, the youngest of whom was a shy little girl named Lydia. With my father's help, the believers dug a well and built a fine wooden parsonage on ten-foot high mahogany posts.

By 1964, the war between North and South Vietnam was growing increasingly violent. When the United States bombed the Ho Chi Minh Trail on Cambodian soil, Cambodia's king demanded all Americans to leave his country. Three weeks later, we said goodbye to the little group of Christians at Kabal Chua and left Cambodia. Lydia was six years old. None of us had even the slightest inkling about the catastrophe that would eventually engulf the country.

Five years later the Khmer Rouge took over Kratie. They came to the village, arrested Pastor Kru On, marched him fifty yards into the rice field behind his house and shot him in front of his wife and children. Later that week, they burned the church to the ground and gave the property to his neighbors.

Kru On's wife died a few years later. Vietnam eventually sent its army into Cambodia and drove the Khmer Rouge out of power. After the war, all of Kru On's children–except Lydia—abandoned their faith and left the village. For several years, she was the only remaining vestige of Christianity in the village of Kabal Chua.

Lydia eventually married and over the next twenty-five years gave birth to three children, all of whom followed the Buddhist religion. In the mid-90s, Cambodian Christians arrived in the town of Kratie where our family had lived and started a house church. A few years later, an American missionary arrived and preached to large crowds. Nearly one hundred Cambodians turned to faith in Christ, and a few years later, they built the first of two Christian churches in Kratie.

Eventually a team of Christians from Kratie visited in Kabal Chua and held a public service. Several of the listeners, including Lydia, decided to follow Christ and formed a small church. Soon after, Lydia became pregnant and gave birth to another son, one that she was determined to raise as a Christian. She became deeply attached to the boy.

One day in the summer of 2004, her son complained about a sudden, severe headache. A few days later, he developed a high fever and died. Lydia was devastated. She felt betrayed by God and was overwhelmed with sorrow. For months she could hardly do her work. Her husband became angry with her, especially after his Buddhist relatives and neighbors suggested that the boy had died because of Lydia's faith. Lydia's neighbors came to "comfort" her by urging her to give up her faith in Christ. After all, hadn't the Christian God she had trusted failed to protect her son?

The small group of believers in Kabal Chua tried to encourage Lydia and pray with her, but she could not stop thinking that God had let her son die. To their dismay, she agreed to a Buddhist funeral for her son. Afterwards, she slid into a profound depression.

Two weeks after Lydia's son died, my wife Becki and I arrived in Kratie with our daughter Rachael. I had been away for thirty-nine years and didn't even remember Lydia. A young Christian named Srung agreed to take us to Kabal Chua to see what was left of the church.

There were many more houses in Kabal Chua than I remembered. Where the church had once stood there was now a house. The parsonage was still where I had last seen it, next to the well that my father had helped the Christians dig by hand back in 1958. So much had changed that the place was difficult to recognize.

As Srung led us towards the old parsonage, we saw a small, thin, middle-aged woman standing at the bottom of the stairs leading up to the front porch. She looked surprised and frightened, but as Srung greeted her and politely explained in Cambodian that we were the children of the missionaries who had worked with her father, her hand flew to her mouth and her eyes widened in astonishment. She blurted out something to Srung in Cambodian, and Srung turned to us and explained that this was Lydia, Kru An's youngest daughter. I was too overcome with surprise and emotion to do anything but greet her in Cambodian. Lydia invited us up onto her porch and explained that her husband was working in his rice fields.

Our daughter, Rachael, is fluent in Cambodian, so for the next hour she translated Lydia's words for us. We sat on the porch floor, as is customary for visitors, and for the next hour answered Srung's questions about our family. She had heard that the Viet Cong in Banmethuot had killed my parents in 1968, and afterwards she had cried for a long time. Then she described all that had happened to her family. As she talked, tears rolled down her cheeks and dripped onto the floor.

When she came to the end of her story, Srung asked her if he could tell us about the death of her son. She stiffened and turned her head, but after a moment turned back and nodded. Srung told us the story of how he had died, and soon tears were filling our eyes. I decided to tell her my own story.

For the next hour, I shared what God had done in my life and in the lives of my brothers and sisters. I explained how at first I had been furious with God for failing to protect my parents, but then God had spoken to me and challenged me to trust him, even without understanding what he was doing. I told about how I had surrendered my heart to God and had decided to trust in him, even though I didn't understand. God took away my sorrow and replaced it with joy, and in the years that followed, God blessed me and overwhelmed me with his love and kindness. She listened, wiping her eyes often but saying nothing.

In the end, we prayed for God's peace and blessing on Lydia and took pictures of us together by the well. Then we gave her a small gift and left.

Five years later we visited Lydia again. This time when she saw us she smiled and clapped her hands. Her husband had died, and now several of her small nieces lived with her, bringing life and joy into her house. Once again we encouraged her to follow Jesus and left her with a small gift of money to show that we cared about her.

I don't know how Lydia's story will end, but I know for certain that God brought my wife, my daughter and me all the way from central Africa at the very moment of Lydia's greatest pain to tell her that he loved her and had not forgotten her.

Encounters are *never* random, either in the Bible or in real life. They are *always* arranged by God's Spirit.

Divine Interruptions

I once stopped in an African village close to where we often vacationed on the beach. It was Sunday, and I wanted to invite the villagers to a church service. The chief was a woman who had undergone surgery at our hospital. After I explained to her what I wanted to do, she suggested that we meet in her living room. The small house looked as though a strong gust of wind might blow it down around us, but twenty-five people crowded in anyway to hear what we had to say. The people listened attentively as I told the first of many stories that would eventually lead them to know the God of the Bible.

Afterwards, the chief asked if I would go with her to see her sick aunt. I really did not want to go, since I was on vacation and hadn't planned to get involved treating sick people. Besides, I felt like I was already doing God a favor by taking time off from my vacation to preach! I was about to refuse when God quietly told me to go and see the old woman.

I found the chief's aunt in an old wooden kitchen that looked like it was about to fall down. She was lying on a mat on the dirt floor. A small fire bled smoke into the dark room. My eyes started to sting and tear up, and I suppressed a strong urge to rush outside for some fresh air. The woman looked to be about seventy-years-old and was wheezing, probably from pneumonia or heart failure, or maybe just from the smoke! I had a handful of emergency medicines under the seat in my car and was about to go and see what I had to offer her when the Lord said to me, "Pray for her."

What for? I thought to myself. *She's so old she's not going to make it anyway!* But I complied. The old woman didn't understand French, but when I laid a hand on her arm, closed my eyes and began talking to God about her, she knew I was praying. By the time I finished asking God to do what would have to be a major miracle, I was coughing and wiping my eyes, but I stayed until I had told her about Jesus' love for her and how she could believe in him and receive his pardon for her sins.

After we all said "Amen," I told the chief to get her out of the smoke, put her on a salt-free diet, and take the antibiotic pills that I left for her.

Two days later, I was surprised to see the chief's auntie up on her feet and heading down the beach to her garden in the forest to get some manioc from her field! She recovered completely and lived for several more years, which was long enough for her to really understand God's story of forgiveness and grace and put her faith and trust in Jesus.

God arranged that encounter, and because of it an old woman in a tiny village in Central Africa became a child of God.

Jesus was in a similar situation one day when he was on his way to heal an important man's daughter. A woman who had been bleeding for twelve years reached out and touched his clothing as he went by, hoping to be healed. The disciples were ready to scold the woman, but when Jesus saw her, he said, "Daughter, be encouraged! Your faith has made you well!" And she was healed at that moment.[31] Jesus recognized it was a divinely appointed encounter and did exactly what his Father wanted him to do.

For Jesus, these incidents were not interruptions that delayed him from doing something more important. They were appointments arranged by his father, opportunities to teach his future children how to believe in him.

We are mistaken if we think that God's Spirit is tied to the appointments on our calendars. God has his own schedule for our days, and when he interrupts us he expects us to stay cool, pay attention, and respond with mercy and compassion.

Encounters in the Bible

The Bible describes thousands of events, meetings, incidents, and encounters between people, events that God knew about well in advance. Here are just a few of his statements about encounters (*emphasis* mine):

- "The Lord directs the *steps* of the godly. He delights in every detail of their lives." (Psalm 37:23)

- "We can make our plans, but the Lord determines our *steps*." (Proverbs 16.9)

- "Lord my God, you have performed many wonders for us. Your *plans* for us are too numerous to list. You have no equal. If I tried to recite all your wonderful deeds, I would never come to the end of them." (Psalm 40:5)

We may think that we are running our own show, but again and again God says otherwise:

- "The Lord of Heaven's Armies has spoken—who can change his *plans*? When his hand is raised, who can stop him?" (Isaiah 14:27)

- "And the Lord said, 'That's right, and it means that I am watching, and I will certainly carry out all my *plans.*'" (Jeremiah 1:12)

- "'I know the *plans* I have for you,' says the Lord. 'They are plans for good and not for disaster, to give you a future and a hope.'" (Jeremiah 29:11)

When God called Saul to become Israel's first king, he had Samuel explain to the young man exactly what would happen to him later that same day: "When you arrive at Gibeah of God. . . . you will meet a band of prophets coming down from the place of worship. They will be playing a harp, a tambourine, a flute, and a lyre, and they will be prophesying. At that time the Spirit of the Lord will come powerfully upon you and you will prophesy with them" (1 Sam 10:5-6). And that's exactly how it turned out.

In the book of Samuel, the story is told of how God kept David and his men from taking vengeance against a man named Naboth who insulted them. As the men rode to battle, Naboth's wife Abigail intercepted them with a generous gift of food and an apology. He said to her, "Praise the Lord, the God of Israel, who has sent you to meet me today!" (1 Sam 25:32). David knew that it was not a chance encounter.

When Jesus needed a donkey to ride into Jerusalem, he sent his disciples ahead with these instructions: "Go into the village over there," he said. "As soon as you enter it, you will see a donkey tied there, with its colt beside it. Untie them and bring them to me. If anyone asks what you are doing, just say, 'The Lord needs them,' and he will immediately let you take them." (Luke 19:30)

This event was predicted more than four hundred years before in Zechariah 9:9: "Tell the people of Israel, 'Look, your King is coming to you. He is humble, riding on a donkey—riding on a donkey's colt." The disciples Jesus sent to fetch the donkey colt found things exactly as he had told them and brought it to him to ride into the city of Jerusalem. (Luke 19:31-34) God can even arrange our encounters with animals!

There are so many more examples in the Bible of God's planning for the events that it would take too long to describe them all. The point they all make is that our daily encounters with people are not random, but carefully planned by our Heavenly Father. If those we encounter need help, God intends for us to respond with the truest kind of mercy.

Chapter 5

ONLY ONE HEALER

"Then I will not make you suffer any of the diseases I sent on the Egyptians; for I am the Lord who heals you."

Exodus 15:6b

The Midwives of Healing

This week I received an email that warmed my heart. A five-year-old Malian girl first brought to our hospital in Gabon for a heart defect underwent successful corrective surgery at the Mayo Clinic—at no cost to her family.

Her surgery was successful for a variety of reasons, including the fact that she had a correctable defect, did not have irreversible damage to her lungs from the abnormal blood flow in her heart, had an American pediatrician championing her case with the cardiologists and surgeons at Mayo clinic for almost two years, was able to undergo a sophisticated diagnostic cardiac echogram in Gabon, and received a free round-trip ticket to the United States from Air France. In addition to all that, Mayo Clinic had some of the world's most skilled pediatric cardiologists, cardiac surgeons, anesthesiologists, critical care nurses, respiratory therapists, and laboratory technicians working on her. The surgery was flawless and the results were excellent.

It would seem perfectly logical to conclude that this little girl was healed by the doctors, nurses, and medical technicians who helped her. But it would not be the truth. Why is that? *Because the Bible teaches that Jesus is the author of all healing, whether natural, medically-assisted, or supernatural.*

I once operated on a four-year-old girl suffering from a swollen and tender knee. An X-ray showed normal appearing bones and what looked like multiple, small abscesses in the soft tissues under the skin and around her knee joint. I assumed she had an infection that simply needed to be drained and treated with antibiotics. In the operating room the next day when I opened her knee and looked inside, I was surprised when I did not find pus in either the swollen soft tissue around her knee or in her knee joint. Puzzled, I washed out the joint, sewed up the small incisions I had made, and treated her with antibiotics.

Ten days later, the wounds around her knee showed no signs of healing and her knee was even more painful than before. Thinking the sutures might be irritating the wound, I took them out. The next day her incisions fell open as if we had made them the day before. One month later she was still not better and we were trying to find out why her wounds would not heal.

Several specialists came to our hospital during that time, but all of them were as puzzled as we were. We tried a variety of treatments, including the treatment for tuberculosis. None of them helped.

During this time, my residents and I prayed often for the little girl when we made rounds. It was difficult to see her each day because of her suffering. A day came when we had to make a difficult choice: amputate her leg above the knee or simply let her go home the way she was. I asked our surgical team to gather around and lay hands on her. I said in my prayer, "Father, we don't know what to do here. We've tried everything we know, and nothing has worked. We don't want to amputate her leg, but we don't know what else to do. You are the one who has given us the knowledge that we have, the medicines that we use, and the knowledge to use them. But right now we've run out of knowledge. Please show us what to do or touch this little girl with your hand of healing and make her better. We ask this in the name of Jesus Christ, Amen."

There was a little silence when I finished, and then somebody asked if this could possibly be an infection caused by a rare bacterium that can cause deep wounds that burrow under the skin and deeper. I looked at the ugly, swollen, draining knee and the crying girl and thought about it. I had treated at least one hundred of those infections in the past thirty years, but I had never seen or read about such an infection invading a major joint without first ulcerating the skin. That kind of infection was caused by a germ called *Mycobacterium ulcerans.* We had no way to test for it, so we would have to make an educated guess. We had nothing to lose except more time and money, so we decided to give her the recommended treatment for *Mycobacterium ulcerans.* Given the choice between an amputation, going home without resolution of the problem, or our proposed treatment, the mother chose to stay a few weeks longer.

Four weeks later, that little girl walked out of the hospital on her own two legs, her knee almost completely healed. You could say that we guessed right, but these kinds of things happen so often at our hospital that I think God drops ideas into our minds when we ask for help. After all of our fumbling around, it was God who gave us the right diagnosis at the right time.

It does not matter how far you go into the science of wound healing, cell biology, microbiology, biochemistry, or even quantum physics, you and I do not have to instruct a muscle or joint capsule cell to do what it was made to do. It already knows. This fact is beautifully illustrated by the introductory sentence from Chapter 1 of

Schwartz's eighth edition of Principles of Surgery:

> *The inflammatory response to injury and activation of cellular processes are inherently designed to restore tissue function and eradicate invading microorganisms. Local injuries of limited duration are usually followed by functional restoration with minimal intervention. By contrast, major insults to the host are associated with an overwhelming inflammatory response that, without appropriate and timely intervention, can lead to multiple organ failure and adversely impact patient survival.*[32]

In the case of a "major insult" to the body, all that we as physicians, nurses, and surgeons can do is to *help* the human body heal itself. We may call that healing and we may even take full credit for it, but in reality we are like the clever midwives who safely deliver babies.

One of the first and most important lessons that I learned in my general surgery residency was the importance of draining pus. We drain pus from abscesses almost every day at our hospital, and within hours of that procedure our patients start to improve. Their fevers drop, their pain decreases, their appetites return, they start to smile and laugh again, and they grow stronger by the hour. It works because it shifts the balance of power from the infection to the body's immune system. It is sometimes difficult to find the pus or safely drain it. We can take a little credit for the skills involved, but the One who gave mankind the idea to drain pus from the body in the first place was God. He is also the One who showed the first anesthesiologist and all who followed the drugs that we use so casually in hospitals all over the world today so that patients don't have to be tied down with ropes and gagged to tolerate the pain of surgery. You could say that those thousands and even millions of serendipitous moments when those discoveries were made simply happened, but you would be guessing. Even the scientific method was an idea, and it led to the discovery of millions of scientific facts.

The Gift of Knowledge

We have already talked about the fact that no single human being is capable of learning all the medical knowledge there is to know in the world. One human cannot even master the knowledge learned on earth in just one year. The number of research articles published each year in scientific journals may exceed one-hundred thousand, and at the time I'm writing this there are more than 283 million scientific articles listed on the Internet. Without exception, these discoveries describe things that already existed in our universe and world.

There is a famous story about ten blind men encountering a rather tame elephant. One ran his hand along the elephant's trunk and concluded that the elephant was like a python. Another wrapped his arms around one of the animal's legs and declared that it was like a tree trunk. A third one felt the elephant's massive abdomen and concluded that it was like a wall, and so on. Their description of the elephant was false until they put together what each of them had learned. However, because they were all blind, none of them realized that the elephant was gray. That "blindness" is a commentary on the limitations of what we can learn with our senses and through logic and research. These tools are wonderful, but they are incapable of discovering the spiritual world and understanding its impact on our lives.

The Bible says in Colossians 1:15-17:

Christ is the visible image of the invisible God. He existed before anything was created and is supreme over all creation, for through him God created everything in the heavenly realms and on earth. He made the things we can see and the things we can't see. . . . Everything was created through him and for him. He existed before anything else, and he holds all creation together.

Hebrews 1:2b-3 states the same thing in different terms: "God promised everything to the Son as an inheritance, and through the Son he created the universe. The Son radiates God's own glory and expresses the very character of God, and he sustains everything by the mighty power of his command."

Daniel 2:21 states the truth that God is the author and giver of all knowledge unequivocally: "He controls the course of world events; he removes kings and sets up other kings. He gives wisdom to the wise and knowledge to the scholars."

Hebrews 11:3 says, "By *faith* we understand that the entire universe was formed at God's command, that what we now see did not come from anything that can be seen" (*emphasis* mine).

You cannot be a serious follower of Jesus Christ and believe that the world just happened by chance over billions of years and that we are the products of chance. We may not agree on how it all happened, but God has stated unequivocally in his Word that *he* is the one who created the universe and our world, *he* is the one who sustains it and keeps it going. Just because we are capable of understanding vast amounts of scientific knowledge about our universe does not give us the right to claim credit for what happens. Knowledge about God and about the universe is a gift from the Creator, and he has granted it to us because he wants us to work with him as partners.

Let me return to the story about the little girl with the *Mycobacterium ulcerans* infection of the knee. The antibiotics we administered for her infection entered her blood stream and were taken everywhere in the body, including her infected knee. Because they were the right ones for that mysterious infection, they stopped those bacteria from reproducing, weakened their cell membranes, allowed armies of infection-fighting white cells to destroy the weakened germs and clean up their debris, and freed the tissues that make up the knee joint to heal and close the wound.

We treated this little girl with knowledge that God gave us and to the scientists who produced the medications. Not only did God drop the idea into one of our minds that fateful day, but the entire treatment protocol we used was based on knowledge granted by God to researchers decades ago. He did not give it to them so they would become famous, but for the express purpose of helping sick and suffering children. That is just one small example of the kind of partnership God desires to have with those who believe in him.

The process of healing was created by a master designer whose knowledge is complete and inexhaustible. Check out any one of the current major textbooks on the healing mechanisms of the human body and try to read through it in less than a month. To completely master what we know today about the subject would take the average person three to five years, depending on how bright he or she is—and by then there will probably be twice as much to know!

The healing processes of the body were not designed like a Swiss watch that is set spinning in the factory and left to wind down and stop. A watch would be simple by comparison, and unlike a watch that cannot fix itself, the Creator empowered our bodies to fix themselves for countless breakdowns.

There are times, however, when injuries or infections can be so great that they overwhelm our intrinsic capacities to heal without outside help. It is then that God invites us to partner with him by using both the knowledge he has given us and his power. To physicians who acknowledge God's lordship, believe in his limitless power, and are not too proud to ask for his help, God can be an especially attentive and powerful partner.

Healed by Figs?

There are many examples in the Bible where God invited an individual to partner with him in a miracle. We have already mentioned the story found in 2 Kings 20 when King Hezekiah had a fatal illness. At the beginning of the account, the prophet Isaiah came with a message for the king: "Set your affairs in order, for you are going to die. You will not recover from this illness." As Isaiah walked out of the palace, Hezekiah turned to God and begged him to let him live. God heard his prayer and told Isaiah to turn around and give the king another message: because God had heard his prayer and seen his tears, he would allow him to live another fifteen years. After he delivered the message, Isaiah turned to the king's servants and said, "Make an ointment from figs and spread it over the boil, and Hezekiah will recover." They did, and King Hezekiah recovered from the illness that was killing him.

So what healed Hezekiah? God or the figs? Those of us with medical training immediately start thinking that Isaiah must have added the fig paste on his own. Perhaps it was his favorite home remedy, and it probably had nothing to do with the boil healing. After all, boils do not usually kill people and sometimes they drain on their own, regardless of what you put on them.

I can tell you that the treatment of boils is not all that complicated. I have lanced thousands of them in my career as a surgeon. But I have never heard of a case of fatal boils—or boils that got better after a thick application of fig sauce! Is it possible that King Hezekiah's disease was not really that serious?

The illness that Hezekiah described in his poem of thanksgiving in Isaiah 38 indicates that it was much more than a boil. He said "Suddenly, my life was over. I waited patiently all night, but I was torn apart as though by lions. Delirious, I chattered like a swallow or a crane, and then I moaned like a mourning dove." Isaiah 38:14

If the king had a boil that could be cured with fig paste, why didn't Isaiah suggest it the first time he visited King Hezekiah with a message from God? Why suggest his favorite remedy at the moment that God told him to announce to the king that he would be healed and live another fifteen years? The answer is that the fig ointment was God's idea.

Some might prefer to believe that Hezekiah's healing occurred because of the power of natural medicine. Perhaps there was some secret substance in the fig paste—maybe even penicillin fungus! The only problem with this idea is that fig sauce has never proven itself to be much of a healing substance.

What appears most likely in this story is that Hezekiah was healed by the finger of God *and* the fig sauce. God partnered with Isaiah to heal king, and both elements were necessary to bring it about.

There is a similar story in the book of Exodus, after God and Moses miraculously led the people across the Red Sea on to dry land. God then had Moses lead the Israelites across the desert for three days. When they finally found water, they couldn't drink it because it was bitter. God instructed Moses to throw a piece of wood into the water, and when he complied, the water became sweet. Was it a special wood, or something ordinary? Whatever it was, when Moses did what God commanded him to do, the water became sweet and drinkable.

Conclusion

God is the author of all healing, whether it be accomplished by the systems he has built into our bodies, physician-assisted, supernatural, or any combination of the three. His preferred way of healing is always to do it in partnership with those of us who believe in him and love him.

In the next chapter we will take a look at the one thing we must live by, if we want to please God and receive his help.

Chapter 6
THE RULE OF FAITH

And it is impossible to please God without faith.

Hebrews 11:6

Faith Healing

Jesus commanded his disciples to heal the sick through faith, and there is nothing in the Bible that states that this method has changed. *Jesus expects his followers to heal the sick through faith,* and nowhere did he teach that this command would be null and void if his disciples also used the medical resources and knowledge that God had given them.

Since most of us do not have the faith to heal people and do miracles as seemingly effortlessly as Jesus did, we tend to think that his way of healing people no longer has a place in our modern world. The other extreme in our thinking is that if we use proven medical resources, God will not respond to our prayers for healing.

Just this week, a friend called me to ask my advice about a Christian brother who was suffering from an invasive cancer of his face. As I listened to her, it became clear that none of the different medical modalities we were discussing were capable of healing this man. Our medical resources might keep him alive for another six months, but the disease had already spread beyond our capacities to help him. The only thing we had left were ways in which to help the man die with minimal pain as the cancer invaded his brain. But this man's condition was not hopeless yet, because the God who healed lepers who had lost their fingers and noses and who healed blind people whose eyes were nothing but lumps of scar tissue is still fully capable of healing people of cancer, HIV/AIDS, and other hopeless conditions without the help of doctors—if there is faith.

Jesus made it clear to his followers that he expected them to live and work by the principle of faith, just as he did. To his disciples, he said in John 14:12-14, "I tell you the truth, anyone who believes in me will do the same works I have done, and even greater works, because I am going to be with the Father. You can ask for anything in my name, and I will do it, so that the Son can bring glory to the Father. Yes, ask me for anything in my name, and I will do it." (John 14:12-14).

When Jesus sent out His disciples "he gave them authority to cast out evil spirits and to heal every kind of disease and illness" (Matthew 10:1).

On another occasion when his disciples could not heal a demon-possessed boy, Jesus expressed his frustration that both the people and his disciples had so little confidence in God's power to heal the boy. He then rebuked the demon and drove him out of the boy. When his disciples asked him privately why they could not do what he had done, he replied, "You don't have enough faith. I tell you the truth, if you had faith even as small as a mustard seed, you could say to this mountain, 'Move from here to there,' and it would move. Nothing would be impossible." (Matthew 17:20)

The problem is not that God's Spirit has grown weaker, but that our faith in his ability to heal cancer, or AIDS, or psychological illness has all but disappeared. We do not *really* believe that God can do impossible things. He can do *difficult* things, especially if we can see in advance the required steps and he's prepared to do it our way. We are like the people of Nazareth.

When Jesus taught in the synagogue of Nazareth on the Sabbath, his listeners asked, "Where did he get all this wisdom and the power to perform such miracles?" Then they scoffed, "He's just a carpenter, the son of Mary and the brother of James, Joseph, Judas and Simon. And his sisters live right here among us." They were deeply offended and refused to believe in him. Then Jesus told them, "A prophet is honored everywhere except in his own hometown and among his relatives and his own family." *And because of their unbelief, he couldn't do any mighty miracles among them*, except to place his hands on a few sick people and heal them. (Mark 6:4-5 *emphasis* mine).

This is an astonishing statement, because by this time Jesus had already performed many miracles, miracles that had never been seen in Israel! Yet he told the people of Nazareth that he *could not* heal them. Their lack of faith made it impossible.

Unfortunately, most of the time it is not just we medical professionals who lack faith; those who ask our help for their diseases don't have faith in God's ability to heal them either. But unless we have faith, how can we encourage others to believe? If we aren't willing to bring up the subject of healing to our patients, why should they take the risk of insulting us?

The kind of unbelief demonstrated by the Nazarenes is now the norm in our world and the norm in most of our churches. Let me ask you this: if you were dying of cancer, would you call the elders of your church and ask them to anoint you with oil and pray for you? Would you make the effort to organize an all night prayer meeting and fast for your child's healing? Some might, but the reality is that very few of us are willing to go that far.

Jesus taught that if you do not think your prayers for someone's healing will make a difference, they won't. If you don't have enough faith to even ask God to do something, He won't do what you're hoping he will. While we may have enough faith to believe that God can heal a small thing like our child's fever or a cold sore that we know will eventually heal on its own anyway, we don't have enough faith to believe that he can heal what's killing us. So we pester God to heal our colds, our headaches, and our operable diseases, but we can't bring ourselves to seriously ask God to heal us when we already know it's impossible.

Jesus made it abundantly clear that it is only when we ask God that he answers our prayers. Talking about asking him to heal is like saying you will talk to your spouse about going on a second honeymoon without ever doing it. It's worse than if you hadn't even brought it up! In Matthew 7:7, Jesus said to his disciples, "Keep on asking and you will receive what you ask." James wrote, "you don't have what you want because you don't ask God for it" (James 4:2b).

Sometimes, we don't ask God for something because we're angry with him. King Asa was a descendant of David and was one of Judah's better kings. Then God sent a prophet to reprove him:

"In the 39th year of his reign, King Asa developed a serious foot disease. Yet even with the severity of his disease, he did not seek the Lord's help but turned only to his physicians. So he died in the forty-first year of his reign" (2 Chronicles 16:12-13). Had King Asa asked, God would have healed him! How often does that happen today?

I have often asked God to help me do better surgery or help my patients survive a difficult operation. God has responded to those requests again and again, literally hundreds of times. Can I prove it? Not scientifically, I can't. But as the chorus goes, "God said it, and I believe it, and that's good enough for me!" I do know that I cannot get those results with just my own skill and wisdom.

I have asked God to heal fevers and infections, snake bites and comas. I would be lying if I told you that everyone I prayed for was healed. In fact, most of the time my prayers have not produced dramatic miracles. God does not always do what we expect, and I don't know why he doesn't heal when we his children ask him in great faith. But the point I want to make is this: I've never seen God heal someone who did not think God could or would heal him. I must admit however, that I have blind spots: AIDS and incurable cancer. On numerous occasions I have asked God to heal patients who had AIDS or incurable cancer, and he didn't. That's always hard on my faith, and it makes me reluctant to ask again. Maybe it's because I'm not sure he can heal AIDS and cancer! Yet I've seen him heal incurable cancer. I'll describe some of these cases in the next chapter.

The bottom line is that if we do not ask, God will not give us what we need. If we ask often, he will give it to us sometimes, if it's his will. Our willingness to ask, and ask often, is a sign of our faith in God.

Prayer . . . or Doctors?

The Bible does not state that physicians are a general waste of time and money, although there are a few examples of that. Most of the time Jesus and the apostles were complimentary of physicians. Luke the physician was one of Paul's closest companions. The apostle Paul referred to him in Colossians 4:14 as "Luke, the beloved doctor." Jesus, the greatest healer of all time, once said to his disciples, "It's not the healthy who need a doctor, but the sick." (Matthew 9:12). He wasn't making a point about doctors, but responding to the criticism of the Pharisees that he was spending too much of his time with sinners. Jesus did not belittle doctors.

I am convinced that because of his compassionate nature, God calls people to take up the practice of medicine. Otherwise, he would not have been so generous in giving mankind such detailed knowledge about the human body and the way it works, knowledge about health, disease, and our ability to develop increasingly sophisticated medical technology and treatments. The world's medical knowledge continues to grow exponentially because God created us with the intelligence to understand complex truths and create technology. God made us curious about his creation, and God is generous in sharing his knowledge. We've already seen how modern scientific inquiry developed in Europe beginning in the seventeenth century because of the Christian faith.

It is God who has given human beings the capacity to learn so much about medicine—so much of it that no single physician can master it all. In order to preserve that knowledge and catalogue it in a way that we can access it, mankind has been forced to divide science and medicine into hundreds of specialty and subspecialty areas.

Only when teams of specialists in different fields work together can they apply the vast knowledge God has given them and intervene for good in the human body. We have had to develop enormous libraries to hold printed books and journals, and now we have even greater storage reserves of medical knowledge accessible on the Internet. Despite these impressive advances in our medical knowledge, God never intended that the knowledge he gave us would replace our faith in him.

Today, most of the medicine practiced in the world is practiced without reference to God. Our educational systems teach that the sick have no need for God, unless it is to comfort them with words they might want to hear. Prayer to God for healing is tolerated because of its psychological benefits, not because of its perceived power to heal.

Prayer-Assisted Healing

The worldwide spread of secular medicine would not be so serious if Christian caregivers did not themselves believe that prayer is a useless exercise. While some might dispute this statement, I would ask why do Christian physicians pray so rarely for their patients? Some Christian health workers are embarrassed when their colleagues pray for patients in the office, in the operating room, on the hospital wards, or in the ICU. Some are alarmed that it might be unethical, and speak out against the practice.

There is far more to this attitude than meets the eye. When we act on behalf of our patients without prayer, we are making the following statement: *healing depends entirely on our knowledge, skill, and resources, and whatever ability the patient has to heal himself.* This means that a patient seeking help must place his faith entirely in himself and in his physician. God is . . . well, irrelevant. The same principle is true for relief workers, or those who try to help people with development projects, or counselors, or any other kind of compassion ministry. The outcome depends entirely on the knowledge, skill and resources of the people in charge and the people being helped.

In contrast to the faithless healer, the caregiver who prays for his patient invites God's *direct* involvement. If the patient agrees to this prayer also, God is free to intervene powerfully in the sick person's body, soul and spirit. In the same way, the program director for a relief or development project who prays for the people he is trying to help and to the extent possible enlists them in praying, opens the door for God to work powerfully and in ways that cannot always be explained or even perceived.

God's plan for people who are sick or suffering is not simply to enable them to live for another week, or month, or even five years. His plan for them is to help them in their suffering and then adopt them into his own family (Ephesians 1:5). He wants people to be healthy and to have their needs met while on earth, but he also wants them to live with him forever in the best place in the universe: heaven!

The caregiver who prays for his patient is saying to God and to his patient that— as a professional—he is not enough. He requires God's help. This opens the door for God to pour out his power in multiple ways.

On the basis of Hebrews 11:6, the caregiver, the relief worker, or the project manager who does not sincerely and earnestly ask for God's help and intervention in what he does to help those who suffer, who does not expect God to intervene supernaturally, who does not demonstrate his faith in God's ability to make a difference in what he is doing, should not think that God will lift a finger to help him. When we omit God from our good deeds to help others, we make certain that the success or failure of our project depends entirely on our own efforts. If even our most strenuous and sacrificial efforts amount to nothing, if we did not ask God to help us we have no reason to be disappointed with him.

What God wants to do is to work in *partnership* with us, to alleviate human suffering and bring new life to people. He wants to build our faith to dizzying heights and multiply our efforts a thousand-fold. But he will do it only if we follow his lead and his teachings.

What's Left to Decide?

There may be another reason that Christians would rather act than pray: they can't figure out what prayer is. Of course, we all know that prayer is "talking with God," but it still doesn't make sense.

Here's the scenario: God is up in heaven doing his thing, ruling the cosmos, holding everything together, ordering events on earth, and making things happen his way. According to the Bible, God rules over the good angels, the bad angels (demons), and even the devil. Not only that, he alone knows everything that will happen ahead of time. Ephesians 1:4 says, "Even before he made the world, God loved us and chose us in Christ to be holy and without fault in his

eyes. God decided in advance to adopt us into his own family ..."
It seems clear that everything has already been decided by God.

That impression grows stronger as one reads through the book of Revelation. In chapter after chapter, we read about the fall of kings and kingdoms, coming plagues, firestorms, battles, severe persecution, and at long last, the return of Christ. What is the point of asking God to change things that have already been set in stone? How can prayer be considered as anything more than an exercise in futility? The God of the Bible not only knows everything and holds all power in his hands; he is *unchangeable*. Asking him to change his perfect plans is absurd, so why would he listen to us? If he did what I asked, like move a mountain or allow someone to live another fifteen years, would that not upset his carefully laid plans set in motion ages ago?

If you thought the plot of *Back to the Future III* was wild, imagine what would happen if *one million* people asked God for special favors, all at the same time, and he granted them? Wouldn't there be utter chaos? Unless—and this is a really big "unless"—an all-knowing God *planned* for prayer, and the possibility that all of his children would ask him for special favors all the time, some of which he would be delighted to grant. That could only work if God had *two or more* plans for every scenario, for every possible event: one in case we asked him to do something, and another one if we did not. Plan A, Plan B, and more plans!

It turns out that the Bible and life are full of Plans A, B, and more.

The Day the Earth Reversed Direction

In Chapter 5 we told King Hezekiah's story of and how at first God told him he was going to die. But after Hezekiah prayed to God and asked him for healing, God answered his prayer and promised him another fifteen years of life. We pick up the story in 2 Kings 20:9, where God said to Hezekiah through the prophet Isaiah, "This is the sign from the Lord to prove that he will do as he promised. Would you like the shadow on the sundial to go forward ten steps or backward ten steps?" God's preferred plan for Hezekiah was not an afterthought, a reluctant concession to a faithful king, but a plan that God had prepared in advance and that involved a stunning miracle. God asked Hezekiah to decide how the miracle would happen!"

Hezekiah asked God to move the sun ten steps *backward* on the sundial because it would be the harder thing for God to do. His decision was not a challenge to God, but a demonstration of his faith in God's power. As such it could only have pleased God, and it could only happen if the earth either reversed direction or made a violent wobble. It was an event so astounding that the next year astrologers from Babylon came to Jerusalem to try and figure out what had happened. Because Hezekiah's choice required greater faith, God was clearly pleased.

Did a giant meteor hit the earth at that precise moment or did some other cataclysmic event occur? We don't know, but no matter what happened, God would have had to prepare the event far in advance to make it happen. If King Hezekiah had not prayed his prayer of faith, the miracle would not have happened, and I think God would have been disappointed!

Can We Make It Work?

How do we, as medical practitioners caring for desperately ill patients and relief and development workers helping those who suffer, enlist the finger of God for others? The answer is simple: we must ask, and we must keep on asking. How often do we pray for those we are helping? Out loud? In their presence? Even silently as we help them?

Of course, you can get into serious trouble for praying aloud for someone you are helping, especially if you live in the United

States and the person is not an evangelical Christian. A friend of mine who is a board-certified gynecologist recently experienced this situation, after caring for a woman who claimed to be a follower of Christ. She was suffering from painful uterine bleeding, was past the childbearing age, and wanted something done to stop her bleeding. He proposed a hysterectomy to stop her bleeding. After listening to all the pros, cons, and risk of what could go wrong, she agreed to the procedure. Since she professed to be a Christian, my friend said he would like to pray for her. She agreed, and he prayed a short prayer for her in his office, asking for God's divine protection and blessing on the operation. Six months later, she sued him—not for performing incompetently or negligently but—for "coercing her through prayer!" Fortunately, the case was thrown out before it came to trial.

Let's assume, for the sake of discussion, that we are talking about a Christian hospital somewhere in the developing world. It's a place where people—even Muslims—do not get upset when you ask them if you can pray before you give them an anesthetic for an operation, or after you consult them in the office.

Imagine that you are a physician and are called to the emergency room to see a twenty-eight-old man who has just vomited a large amount of blood. His blood pressure is 60/0 and he is in profound shock. When you arrive, you notice that your patient is lying very still, although his eyes are open and he is looking at you sleepily. The nurses have started an IV, and fluid is pouring into his veins. Someone is checking his blood pressure every few minutes, and as you begin to question the patient and his anxious parents, a lab tech shows up and sticks the patient's finger for a blood test.

The story that emerges is that the young man has been a heavy drinker for the past ten years. He first vomited blood two weeks ago at home. A doctor he consulted told him to stop drinking alcohol, so he did. He assures you that he has not touched alcohol for two weeks. As he says this, you notice that his mother looks out the window and his father looks at the floor.

The nurse attending to the patient announces that his blood pressure is now 100/60. The lab tech returns and shows you the lab report. The young man's blood count is a third of what it should be. You ask which member of the family wants to be tested first to see if they can give blood. The boy's mother volunteers and heads off to the laboratory.

You examine the patient and discover that his abdomen is full of fluid. This is not good, because it probably means that the young man has cirrhosis of the liver. The blood that normally flows back to the heart from his stomach, spleen and all his intestines can no longer filter through the liver. Instead, the blood has to push its way under high pressure around the liver through veins that line the esophagus. Because of the high pressure, those veins in the esophagus are likely to be the size of your little finger (called varices). One of them probably ruptured two weeks ago and bled for several hours, and soon another one will probably rupture again and bleed massively.

In America and Europe, there would be a wide selection of procedures one could choose from to help the young man. In Africa, there are only a few, and they are not very good. If you confirm by endoscopy that the young man has esophageal varices, he will still likely die within a few weeks or months.

You explain all this to the family members and the young man. He could bleed again at any time, and the next time it could be fatal. You want to transfuse him some blood so he has some reserves, and later do flexible endoscopy to confirm that he has varices or something else. The transfusion and endoscopy will cost one hundred dollars. The family members blink back a few tears, look at their son with worried looks, and say okay. You head back to operating room and the nurses take the patient to his room.

You have just demonstrated the following:

1. You are a well-trained, Western doctor, perhaps nicer than most.

2. The patient's problem is serious, but you are able to deal with the current problem.

3. The patient should have confidence in you and your team.

4. So far, nobody needs God to do anything.

Are you okay with this? If not, *you will need to explain God's role to your patient and encourage his family to pray and expect God to act!* So let's try this scenario again.

You explain to the family members and the young man that he has a very serious problem caused by years of heavy drinking. He could bleed again at any time and this time it could be fatal. You will need to transfuse some blood so he has reserves if he bleeds again and do flexible endoscopy to see if he has varices or is bleeding from something else in his stomach. Before you can do any of that, however, you would like to ask God to help him. Can you pray for him? (The family and the young man agree readily).

As the doctor in charge, you lay your hand on the boy's arm and pray as clearly as you can so that he and everyone else understand what you are saying as you pray. You thank God for keeping the young man alive until now and ask God in Jesus name to keep him from bleeding again. Then you ask God to give your team wisdom so that you can find out what you need to know about the problem and can give the best treatment. You ask God to help the family find the blood the young man needs and the funds to pay the hospital bill. Then you pray that God will help the young man and his family to understand how much He loves them. You mention that God sent his Son to die for their sins and that he very much wants to them to believe in him and become his own children. Finally, you pray that

God will encourage them and comfort them while they are at the hospital, and will protect the young man from the devil and the evil spirits that want to do him harm (a very big concern in animistic Africa!). You close by asking this in the name of Jesus Christ.

After praying, you ask the young man if he prays to God. He shakes his head, still a bit foggy, but does not seem offended by the question. After that, you tell him that one of our chaplains, a pastor, will be coming by his room to welcome him, greet him, pray for him, and answer any questions he might have.

All of that took less than three additional minutes, and here is what it demonstrated to this family:

1. You are a well-trained doctor who cares about the patient and who relies on God to help you. Your confidence is in God, and you know him personally.

2. The patient's problem is serious. You have a plan to help him; you're asking God to help the young man to be healed.

3. You are concerned about the patient's spiritual state; God loves and cares about the young man, and you want him to meet God personally. Not only that, but by praying to God, you have established that he is the most powerful person in the room.

4. You are asking God to guide you, heal your patient, comfort and encourage the patient and his family, and protect them from Satan and any evil spirits who might want to harm them. You will be asking the chaplain to visit him and pray for him.

Blessing the Sick through Prayer

A colleague of mine who has served most of his surgical career in the military felt God calling him to become a career missionary in Africa. After nine months of studying French in France, he arrived in Africa and found himself teaching African surgery residents at a mission hospital where most of the patients were Muslim. He and his residents were overwhelmed with the work and were uncertain about how to share Christ with their patients. This situation troubled him greatly.

After almost two years, he visited a smaller hospital run by another mission in the same part of the country. To facilitate spiritual conversations with Muslim patients, the hospital had deliberately built all of its new patient rooms to accommodate a single patient. On Thursday evenings, the hospital staff divided into groups that went to every patient's bedside and asked each if they could pray for their healing or any other problems they might have. Nearly every patient agreed to this request. He was amazed at the doors that it opened for discussions at the bedside. He listened to the chaplains, watched how they related to patients, and asked questions about how they shared the gospel with the patients.

When he got back to his hospital, he talked to his residents about doing something similar. They were already meeting each week for a two-hour Bible study and prayer, but they decided to change their schedule and do "prayer rounds" on their patients every other week. At the bedside of each patient the residents explained that they were Christians and had come to ask God to intervene on the patient's behalf.

The surgeons and their wives were amazed at the gratitude and delight most of their patients expressed in response to their prayers for them. Though seventy percent of the patients were Muslims, there were few who declined the offer and none were offended. One night they prayed for a man named Zacharia who had been treated for pulmonary tuberculosis for a long time. The surgical team had treated him twice after his lungs collapsed inside his chest. Now he was back with a large and inoperable mass in his liver and kidney—and he was dying. When the surgeons asked if they could pray for him, Zacharia began to weep. He told them that many years previously he had done something terrible to another person, and now he wanted forgiveness. He had heard the gospel before, but had never trusted Christ personally. That day he prayed to receive Christ and was later baptized.

The surgeon who told me this story commented, "This kind of thing does not happen on clinical rounds every day, but when we are purposeful about coming to the bedside and intervening with God on behalf of the desperately needy people under our care, God opens hearts and doors." This one doctor's determination to follow the teachings of Jesus Christ in his service to the sick impacted the entire hospital. His example will influence the surgeons he is training for the rest of their lives.

Conclusion

Which one of these two individuals represents you? The principle is simple: "Without faith it is impossible to please God." Abandon that principle as you help the sick or those who are suffering and *you are on your own.*

In the next chapter, we will examine how God is able to heal the human body supernaturally, apart from the body's built-in ability to heal itself, with or without the help of physicians.

Chapter 7
SUPERNATURAL HEALING

And Jesus asked them, "Do you believe I can make you see?"
"Yes, Lord," they told him. "We do."
Then he touched their eyes and said, "Because of your faith, it will
happen." Then their eyes were opened, and they could see!

Matthew 9:28-29

D oes our mercy include faith and prayer to heal the sick? Or does its association with spiritual quackery keep us in the world's mainstream?

The question may be especially uncomfortable for Christian medical professionals. For example, we know from our limited experience in North America and Europe that believable reports of people who were supernaturally healed from cancer are hard to find. Few of us have actually seen a miraculous healing. But if we did, would we believe it happened? Would anyone else believe us if we told them that we witnessed a miraculous healing? If we documented it, would our proof be believed?

I am ashamed to say that I myself have at times sent people home to die without even once offering them the opportunity to believe that Jesus could heal them. I doubt very much that I am alone. How merciful are we willing to be to people for whom modern medicine has run out of therapeutic options?

Persisting in Asking

We have already discussed the fact that Jesus healed people with a wave of His hand, by a word, or by touching them. There may still be a few Christians who have a consistent ministry of that kind of healing, although there are enough charlatans around to make it hard to separate the genuine from the fake. There are many Christians, including myself, who could not be considered as miracle workers, but who at one time or another have prayed earnestly for someone to be healed and have seen God do it.

James 5:14 commands Christians to ask for healing: "Are any of you sick? You should call for the elders of the church to come and pray over you, anointing you with oil in the name of the Lord. Such a prayer offered in faith will heal the sick, and the Lord will make you well. And if you have committed any sins, you will be forgiven."

About five years ago, my wife Becki began experiencing dizziness. It got so bad that she could hardly walk. The specialists we consulted confirmed the diagnosis that we had suspected: Becki had a problem with her vestibular organ deep inside the ear that controlled her sense of balance. This amazing and complex little organ is what keeps us from falling down when we are standing, walking, and moving—even when our eyes are closed. The specialists gave us detailed treatment plans to try to reposition the tiny little "rocks" inside the vestibular organ that roll around on top of tiny nerve hairs whenever we move. The nerve hairs tell our brains which way is up, which way is down, and in what direction we are moving. The exercises the specialists recommended required Becki to repetitively drop her head into certain positions to get the little rocks back to where they belonged. This treatment helps some who suffer from this disease, but it did not help Becki. The specialists we consulted also recommended different medications, which are known to be effective, but none of them worked for Becki.

After a month of this, we asked several African pastors and missionaries to anoint Becki with oil and pray for her healing. Though we had high hopes, there was no change. Months passed, and Becki struggled to do even the simplest tasks around the house. She could not drive, could not walk without holding onto things, and lost her appetite. A second time we asked church leaders and missionaries to anoint her and pray for her healing, and again nothing happened. We began to think that it might be God's will for Becki to learn to live with the problem.

As the months dragged on, Becki lost weight, and I became increasingly concerned. We wrote to our supporters and asked them to continue praying for Becki's healing.

About six months after the dizziness started, Becki and I were in the capital city of Gabon. Our daughter Rachael had come to visit us for a month, and it was time for her to fly back to the States. Our missionary colleagues invited us to a farewell party they were holding for two families that would be leaving Gabon to serve elsewhere. We wanted to say goodbye to our friends, so despite Becki's dizziness, we accepted the invitation.

I helped Becki get her food and find a chair under a shady tree in the back yard. We were sitting there talking with our friends when during a break the Lord said to me, "Ask me again." I was not sure if it was the Lord who put that thought into my head or not, but I felt as if it was. After the speeches were over, I asked three or four of our friends to come with us into the house, anoint her with oil again and pray for her. They were happy to do so. Somebody found a little cooking oil, put a drop of it on Becki's forehead, and several prayed, asking God to touch her and heal her completely of her dizziness. By this time we wanted this healing so much that tears ran down my cheeks as they prayed. There was no shouting and nothing dramatic, just five people earnestly asking the Father to make Becki better.

After the last amen, we smiled hopefully at each other and rejoined the others for the rest of the evening.

The next morning when Becki woke up, her dizziness was gone! Better yet, it never came back. I don't think God healed her because those who prayed were more righteous or had more faith than the previous ones. I just think that God waited until he saw that we were not going to give up until he healed Becki. Because we persevered, God did what he had always planned to do, but had we not asked again, it probably would not have happened. This willingness to persevere is something that we'll come back to later in this chapter.

Jesus said in Matthew 7:7, "Keep on asking, and you will receive what you ask for. Keep on seeking, and you will find. Keep on knocking, and the door will be opened to you. For everyone who asks, receives. Everyone who seeks, finds. And to everyone who knocks, the door will be opened."

Refusing and Proving

Let me conclude this section with another true story of someone I know personally who was healed.

A number of years ago a mother brought her eight-year-old son Isaac to the hospital because of increasingly severe abdominal pain and visibly enlarged lymph nodes in his neck. The disease had appeared several months previously and was advancing rapidly. On physical examination, I found that he had enlarged lymph nodes in his neck, under his arms, and in his groin. His liver and spleen were significantly enlarged. An ultrasound of his abdomen revealed tumor-like growths within his liver and spleen. We did not have a CT scanner and his mother could not afford to take her son to the capital city for one, so we offered to perform a small exploration of his abdomen. His mother accepted, so we took the boy to surgery.

What we found was a disseminated lymphoma that was impossible to remove surgically. The diagnosis was confirmed by a biopsy. The boy recovered from the surgery, went home ten days later, and came back two weeks later for a follow up visit. By this time his muscles were wasting, and he was considerably weakened.

At the end of my examination, the mother asked me if Isaac was going to get better. I hesitated a moment, but then decided that she needed the unvarnished truth. "Mama," I said as gently as I could, "there is nothing more we can do for your son. But I can give you the name of an oncologist in Libreville who can treat him with powerful medicines." She shook her head, and as she explained that the family had no money to send the boy to the capital city, tears ran down her cheeks. Her desperation gave me hope, so I asked her, "Do you believe that Jesus can heal your son?"

I knew that she had heard the gospel from the hospital's chaplains and from members of our staff during her son's hospitalization, and that she had not become a believer. So I was a little surprised when she nodded and said, "Yes! Please, please pray that Jesus would heal my son!" So I did, with all the faith I could muster.

Afterwards I said to her, "After you get back home, I want you to talk to Jesus every day and plead with him to heal your son. Will you do that?" She nodded her head emphatically. I gave her pain medication for her son and an appointment to return in one month.

A month went by, and the woman did not return. After two months I concluded that God had not healed the boy and that he had died. Six months passed and I forgot about him entirely.

One day, as I was unlocking my office door at the hospital, a woman came up behind me and asked if she could talk to me. Without turning around, I told the woman that I couldn't see her unless she had an appointment. She continued to plead with me as I entered the door, so I turned and explained that I could not see her before seeing the scheduled patients. She interrupted me and said, "But doctor, this is my son that Jesus healed!" There behind her stood a healthy looking nine-year-old boy. He had grown at least an inch and gained ten pounds, and as I stared at him it hit me: this was Isaac, the boy with the lymphoma that I had prayed for!

I immediately brought the two of them into the office and asked the mother to tell me what happened. She explained that after they had returned home, she had prayed each day for Jesus to heal her son, without fail. A week later he started to feel better. She had not been able to get enough money together to return to the hospital until now. As she told her story, tears streaming from her eyes, I wept with her.

If we don't ask, we shouldn't expect Jesus to heal. And sometimes, when God is pleased with our faith, he answers even the most unlikely prayers.

What God is Looking For

Isaac's story illustrates three important aspects of faith that are often found in those God heals supernaturally. The first is an almost *dogged pursuit of healing* by those who see it. The second is that *we must actually believe in God's ability to heal us*. The third is that God rewards *those who are willing to test their healing.*

Very often in my experience (though not always!) it has been *those who persevered in asking*, despite many discouraging events, who were healed. God will not be manipulated, but his love and compassion for his children is very great.

An example of the first aspect of faith is found in Mathew 15:30: "A vast crowd brought to him people who were lame, blind, crippled, those who couldn't speak, and many others. They laid them before Jesus, and he healed them all."

As we read these accounts, we tend to gloss over how difficult it was for people to find where Jesus was at any given moment, gain access to him through the massive crowds, and bring people to him who were lame, blind, crippled, and otherwise handicapped. They did not have modern means of transporting sick people, cell phones, or even wheelchairs. They had to *carry* people to Jesus! The effort and faith of these families was enormous, and time after time it impressed and moved Jesus.

Compare that to what we are willing to do today to help the sick. How many of us are willing to drive our sick family members to a church at the pastor's request, carry them in on a stretcher or on a wheelchair so that the elders can anoint them with oil and pray for them to be healed? Most of us are willing to drive our sick family members all over town to doctors' offices and to hospitals, even for palliative therapy, but the confidence level for faith in divine healing is so low in American culture that the very idea sounds ridiculous. If that is our attitude, why should Jesus bother to heal us?

A second example is blind Bartimaeus. We read his story in Mark 10: 46b-52:

A blind beggar named Bartimaeus was sitting beside the road. When Bartimaeus heard that Jesus of Nazareth was nearby, he began to shout, "Jesus, Son of David, have mercy on me!"

"Be quiet!" many of the people yelled at him. But he only shouted louder, "Son of David, have mercy on me!" When Jesus heard him, he stopped and said, "Tell him to come here." So they called the blind man. "Cheer up," they said. "Come on, he's calling you!" Bartimaeus threw aside his coat, jumped up and came to Jesus.

"What do you want me to do for you?" Jesus asked.

*"My rabbi," the blind man said, "I want to see!" And Jesus said
to him, "Go, for your faith has healed you." Instantly the man
could see, and he followed Jesus down the road.*

I am always astonished at Bartemaeus' boldness and determination. Jesus had seemingly passed him by, and now people were
telling him to be quiet and that it was too late. The crowds that
thronged around Jesus had to have made it quite difficult for a blind
man to approach him. Bartemaeus didn't care what people thought,
so he shouted repeatedly for Jesus to wait for him, until finally Jesus
heard his voice and called for him to approach. Bartemaeus threw off
his coat—he couldn't have had many of them—and ran to the waiting Jesus. Even then, Jesus wanted to hear from Bartimaeus' own
mouth evidence of his faith, so he asked him what he wanted him to
do. Bartimaeus' answer was the simplest prayer you could imagine:
"I want to see!" but because he had been so dogged in asking Jesus
to help him, Jesus recognized the reality of his faith and did what
he asked.

The second aspect of faith that Isaac's story illustrates, and that
is found often in stories of those God heals in our day, is that *they
actually believe in God's ability to heal them.* Asking God to do
something for us without believing is what the father of John the
Baptist Zechariah did.

Luke 1:6 states that Zechariah and his wife Elizabeth were
"righteous in God's eyes, careful to obey all of the Lord's commandments, and regulations." However, when the angel Gabriel appeared
to Zechariah and announced to him that their prayers had been
answered, he replied, "How can I be sure this will happen?" God did
not change his mind, but because of his unbelief Gabriel reproved
him and made Zechariah mute until his son was had been born and
in obedience he had named his son John. Many of us who grew up
in the church and are following Christ to the best of our ability might

be equally skeptical should God announce his intention to supernaturally heal us in response to our prayers.

In Luke 11:5-10, Jesus taught his disciples these principles in the parable of a man who needed to borrow three loaves of bread from a friend. When the man went to his friend's house at midnight, the friend told him not to bother him, since he and the family were already in bed. But because the man kept knocking and asking, his friend finally got up and gave him what he asked for. Jesus concluded with this famous verse: "And so I tell you to keep asking, and you will receive what you ask for. Keep on seeking, and you will find. Keep on knocking, and the door will be opened to you. For everyone who asks, receives. Everyone who seeks finds. And to everyone who knocks the door will be opened" (Luke 11:9-10). We tend to quote verse 10 without referring to the parable about persevering in prayer that preceded this teaching.

The third aspect illustrated in Isaac's story that is often present in others who are healed in our day is that *God rewards those who are willing to test their healing.* To the paralyzed young man whose friends let him down through the roof of the crowded house where Jesus was teaching, he ordered him to "Take up your bed and walk!" (Mark 2:9). Had the young man replied, "I can't! Don't your realize that my legs are paralyzed?" I doubt he would have ever walked.

In the next chapter we will examine the deadliest of all human disorders—an inborn disease that afflicts everyone—and its only cure.

Chapter 8

THE GREATEST NEWS

God has not called us to simply heal people and leave them in their
sin, but to preach to them the gospel of salvation in Jesus Christ.

Decades ago when I was a medical intern, I was assigned to care for an elderly, white-haired man who had advanced cancer of the prostate. He required large doses of narcotics to control his pain, and he knew what we all knew: he was dying.

Back then, hospices for the dying did not exist and many cancer patients spent their last days or weeks in a hospital bed in a private or a semi-private room, depending on their resources. Most days my patient received at least one visitor a day, but the rest of the time he was alone in his room. I felt sorry for him, so whenever I had a few extra minutes, I would drop by to talk with him. Whenever I entered his room, his face would light up with a smile.

I was on duty late one evening when his nurse called and asked me to see him. It turned out he was constipated from all the narcotics we were giving him to control his pain. I wrote an order for a medication that would help him and was about to leave the nursing station when I thought, "Why not keep him company for a few more minutes?" He had seemed lonely, and I had nothing better to do.

The old man looked up in surprise when I re-entered, then waved me to the chair next to his bed. "Got a minute to sit and listen?" he asked. I nodded and sat down. For the next fifteen minutes he told me about his life, his family, his accomplishments, and finally one of his greatest disappointments. "I thought when I retired, I was going to finally enjoy life and finish out my last years having fun," he said sadly, his voice trailing off. "I have all the money I want, but now it doesn't even matter. Hardly anyone from my family comes to see me. I've become a nobody."

I hesitated a moment, wanting very much to help him, but afraid of what my superiors would say. Then I blurted out, "Do you know God?"

He looked over at me with only slight surprise. "You believe in God, don't you?" he said. I nodded. "Okay," he paused, "how can someone know God?"

I talked for the next thirty minutes, starting with the story of Creation in Genesis and ending with Nicodemus's question to Jesus in John chapter 3: "What must I do to be saved?" The old man listened intently, his eyes glistening with tears that threatened to spill down his cheeks. "What did Jesus tell Nicodemus?" he asked quietly when I paused.

I replied, "He told him that to enter God's kingdom he had to be born again." The old man looked at me blankly, clearly not understanding, so I quoted to him the words of the apostle Paul in Romains 10:9: "If you confess with your mouth that Jesus is Lord and believe in your heart that God raised him from the dead, you will be saved."

We talked about what that meant for about fifteen minutes. Then I asked him, "Do you believe that God raised Jesus from the dead?" He said, "Yes." So I asked,

"Would you like Jesus Christ to forgive you of your sins and take in charge of your life?"

He did not hesitate for an instant. "Yes, I do, because I know what you've said is true. I've done many things in my life that I know were wrong and that I'm sorry for. I'm dying and I'm afraid. I believe that Jesus is alive, that he is God's son, and I want him to forgive me!" My heart pounded with excitement as I led the old man in a prayer of faith.

While we were praying with our heads bowed, the door opened and my senior resident walked in. I opened my eyes and looked at him standing in the doorway. The surprise and annoyance on his face said it all: I was in trouble. He turned on his heel and left. When we finished praying, the old man opened his eyes and looked up at me with tears.

"Thank you, young man," he said, his voice husky with emotion. He reached for my hand and squeezed it as firmly as he could. I spent a few more minutes talking with him and congratulating him for his newfound faith. I encouraged him to pray often and to ask God to help him with the pain and suffering he was experiencing, especially since his time was short. In the cabinet next to his bed, I found a Gideon Bible, opened it to the Gospel of John and showed him the book of John to read when he felt up to it. He knew I had to go, so he squeezed my hand goodbye and said again, "Thank you, son. Thank you for helping me!" I was too overcome with emotion to say anything, so I smiled at him and waved goodbye at the door. "I'll see you tomorrow!" I promised.

My senior resident was waiting for me in the nurse's station, a scowl on his face. He pulled me aside and asked, "What did you think you were doing? Do you think you're a chaplain, a priest? Have you forgotten what you're here for?" As calmly as I could, I explained that the old man was dying. I was just trying to encourage him and help him prepare for death.

My resident shook his head in disgust. "Listen to me, and listen carefully. You are an intern. Your job is not to get religious with your patients but to make sure that they get better and for you to learn how to be a proper doctor! That means you need to understand their diseases, make the right diagnosis, and provide the right treatment. If you can't make your patients better, then your job is to make sure they don't suffer unnecessarily. If you're worried about their souls, get a priest to talk to them! Your job description is to be your patient's doctor! Anything else is *not* your job! Do you understand?"

I tried to explain, but he cut me off. "If you do this again, I'll report you to the chief of medicine tomorrow morning when we make rounds!" I was astonished at his attitude and his anger.

"I thought you were a Christian," I said.

"I *am*!" he hissed, glaring at me like I had lost my senses. "But a doctor can't go around talking to his patients about God! It is *not* our role as doctors to convert people to our religion. If your patients need spiritual help, call the chaplain!" With that, he stormed away. I was tempted to call after him and suggest that he talk to the Catholic sisters that ran the hospital, but it seemed wiser to let him go.

The next morning our team of two interns, two junior residents, and one senior resident made rounds with our attending physician. When we approached the old man's room a crowd of people stood in the hallway outside his room. So many were standing in the doorway that we couldn't get in. Apparently my patient had been someone important, and now that the end was near, everyone felt the need to be seen. My senior resident pushed his way into the room to see what was going on and came back a minute later. "There's no point in going in," he explained. "The old man is comatose and won't last much longer." He did not look at me as he walked past and down the hall to the next room.

I tried to look in as I passed by my friend's room, but all I could see were family members crowding around his bed. I suppose I should have been sad, but what I really felt was relief. Because he had believed, I knew I would see him again, and in the best possible circumstances.

I am saddened and troubled when I hear professing Christians object when compassionate caregivers share the good news of Jesus with those they help, whether it is in a hospital setting or in a refugee camp. A Christian professor once told me that preaching Christ to suffering people was "unethical," because the listeners were obliged to respond.

That issue did not seem to trouble Jesus when He taught and then fed his hungry listeners, not once but twice. When some of those he fed began to think that following Jesus could be a ticket to free food, he reproved them. But Jesus never taught his disciples to stop preaching to the people they were helping.

Certainly Christians need to be careful to not link physical and material help with the gospel. But do we really prefer that people die in their sins, ignorant of God's offer to forgive them? If our answer is yes, then we have limited compassion for the people God brings to us for help.

Perhaps another reason some are offended by the gospel is that they themselves have rejected it. They are in the Church for some other reason. Their unspoken belief may be that the kindest thing to do for someone who does not know God is to remain silent about God's offer of salvation and forgiveness to *anyone* who calls on his name.

What God Wants from Sinners

In his book *Christian Mission in the Modern World*, John Stott wrote, "Anything which undermines human dignity should be an offence to us. But is anything so destructive of human dignity as alienation from God through ignorance or rejection of the gospel?"[33]

Many Christians today seem convinced that God will simply pardon unrepentant people for their rebellion when they get to the next life. But there is not a shred of evidence—either in the Bible or in human experience—that confirms this idea. What Jesus did say clearly and unequivocally was that people who believe in him and repent of their sin will be saved.

God states this principle in 2 Peter 3:8: "But you must not forget this one thing, dear friends: A day is like a thousand years to the Lord, and a thousand years is like a day. The Lord isn't really being slow about his promise, as some people think. No, he is being patient for your sake. He does not want anyone to be destroyed, but wants *everyone* to repent" (*emphasis* mine).

In his compassion, God longs for people to believe that he is their Creator and the only true God. The bible says that he wants people to say with their own lips that they believe that Jesus 'is God's one and only Son.

He says in Ephesians 1:5: "God decided in advance to adopt us into his own family by bringing us to himself through Jesus Christ. This is what he wanted to do, and it gave him great pleasure".

The apostle Paul is unambiguous in his statement, "He does not want anyone to be destroyed, but wants everyone to repent." There are three truths here:

- God wants everyone to repent
- Those who do not repent will be destroyed.
- God does not want anyone to be destroyed

In Ezekiel 18:4, God said, "The soul who sins will die." In Hebrews 9:27 he says "each person is destined to die once and after that comes judgment."

Regardless of what claims we might make about our love for God, if we are silent about the gospel when we are given the opportunity to tell lost people about Jesus, we are quietly affirming that God does not mean what he says about the consequences of human rebellion. Our hearts are not compassionate towards lost people, but hardened.

God's "Plan A"

In John 11:26, Jesus said, "Whoever lives and believes in me will never die." He then asked his listeners what he asks us today: "Do you believe this?"

Do you, the reader, believe that people must hear about Jesus Christ before they can believe in him and ask him to forgive their sins? Or do you think that by helping people eat better or live longer we can change God's laws?

The greatest news since time began is not that science and technology are making it possible for CT scanners or MRIs to peer into the recesses of our bodies to find what's wrong with us, or that satellites spinning invisibly above us can transmit images, songs and video footage to every corner of the earth. The greatest news since time began is that God's plan to judge the unrighteous for their sin and send them to the "lake of fire" described in Revelation 20:15 is *not his preference*! Hades, hell, or whatever other term we use with a laugh and a wave of the hand, will not disappear just because we refuse to believe it exists. The news worth shouting—even if it lands us behind prison bars—is that there is a way for sinful man to escape eternal damnation and total separation from God. This is God's favorite plan for humans!

In Ezekiel 22:30, God complained to the prophet, "I searched for someone to stand in the gap in the wall so I wouldn't have to destroy the land, but I found no one."

One can almost hear God's disappointment as He continues: "So now, I will pour out my fury on them, consuming them with the fire of my anger."

It is God's "Plan B" to judge the world for its injustice, its evil, and its rebellion against him. His judgment will go away if we are compassionate and proclaim the gospel so that people believe in him! This is the plan that God *prefers* at every turn of the page. It is the plan that reflects his compassion, his generosity, his beauty, and his love. He longs for people to be restored to perfection!

In John 11:26, Jesus summed it up in just eight words: "He who believes in me will never die." Out of love, God the Father and God the Holy Spirit were willing to crucify God the Son, and the Son was willing to be crucified for sinners.

There is nothing in the universe that God is more passionate about than Plan A, his plan to save mankind and the world. There is only one problem with it: God has mandated that the Good News be proclaimed by human messengers.

Veronica

Veronica arrived at our hospital one night in shock, after someone in another town had scraped a live baby out of her uterus. She was fifteen-years years old, stunningly beautiful, a high school student—and her teacher's lover. Her teacher's solution was to send the girl to a willing doctor and pay for an abortion. Unfortunately, the teacher's love did not extend to accompanying his nearly dead girlfriend to our hospital when she developed complications.

Our surgical team stabilized Veronica with antibiotics and IV fluids, then took her to the operating room and opened her abdomen. We found a ragged, two-inch hole in the anterior wall of her uterus, and a quart of pus. This was her first pregnancy, and since she had not given us permission to remove her uterus, we closed up the hole in her uterus as best we could, washed out her abdomen with several gallons of sterile saline, and put her on our most powerful antibiotics. Our laboratory was not equipped to tell us which antibiotics were the best to control her infection, so we made an educated guess. Several days after she had stabilized, our chaplain told her about Jesus' love for her.

A week after her first operation, Veronica suddenly turned pale and clammy. Her blood pressure fell to 60/0 and her pulse climbed to two hundred beats per minute. These were the classic signs of septic shock, and the most likely source was from her perforated uterus. She reluctantly agreed to let us remove her uterus to control her infection. In the operating room we again washed pus out of her abdomen and removed her now gangrenous uterus. She would never have children, but it was the only way we could save her.

Following the second operation, our chaplain came to Veronica's room and encouraged her to put her faith and trust in Jesus. That day Veronica prayed a prayer of faith and repentance. A week later she unexpectedly went into shock again and died. All of us grieved her tragic death. Our only comfort was that our compassion for her had included the gospel, and Veronica had found forgiveness in Jesus before it was too late.

In Acts 4:12, the apostle Peter declared, "Salvation is found in no one else, for there is no other name under heaven given to men by which we must be saved." If faith in Christ is the only salvation under heaven, why should physicians and nurses who are saved be so reluctant—for "professional reasons"—to tell their patients about it? If we keep the "greatest news" a secret, what will our patients say after they awake in the worst place in the universe? Will they thank us for our thoughtful, compassionate care, or will they curse us for our silence?

A Man with Yellow Eyes

A few years ago a man came to our hospital with yellow eyes. Cancer of the liver is one of the most commonly occurring cancers in Africa, and this turned out to be his diagnosis. The cancer was too advanced to remove surgically, so he lay in his hospital bed for several weeks, dying slowly. I saw him every few days when I made rounds with my residents, and each time I would greet him warmly, ask him how he felt, and listen politely as he told us about his nausea, pain, lack of appetite, progressing weakness, and inability to sleep. All we could do was make him as comfortable as possible. When he talked we would look at his chart, look out the window, even look at the wall—anything but at his unbearably yellow eyes. When our question and answer sessions eventually petered out, we would pat him on the back in sympathy and turn to the next patient.

Several times our chaplains talked to the dying man about Jesus, but he always managed to put them off and delay his decision. Several days before he died, I noticed his wife sitting on a low stool at the end of his bed. She rested her head on her hands, weary with the waiting and dreading the day she would be a widow. There was a hopelessness in her face that made me wonder if the young man's family was not already blaming her for her husband's illness, through sorcery.

As I looked at her, I sensed a deep stillness in my spirit. It was as if all the noise in the room stopped, like the hush of death. I knew that God was speaking to me, but I wasn't sure what he was saying. I looked back at the man and saw what I should have noticed all along—here was someone whose existence would not simply end when his body died.

When we finished checking on the other patient in the room and my residents had filed out, I remained behind. I sat on the young man's bed and asked him if he knew what was going to happen to him after he died. He looked down, shrugged his thin shoulders, and said that no, he didn't really know. I asked him if he knew that God was acutely interested in him, and he looked surprised. For the next fifteen minutes, I explained the gospel to him again in simple terms. I asked him once more if he wanted to join God's family. He had heard it all before, and in his own language, not in French. But because I was his doctor and I was now taking the time to explain it to him again, I think he decided that what I was asking him to do was really important. He said yes, he did want to join God's family, he did believe that Jesus was God's son, and he was willing to follow Jesus and abandon his old way of life. He and his wife prayed to Jesus and asked him to be the Lord of their lives and hearts. Even as the young man's strength faded, that hope in God grew each day as they continued to believe. A week later, the young man died, and I am absolutely certain that his new Father welcomed him with open arms!

"God saved you by his grace when you believed. And you can't take credit for this; it is a gift from God. Salvation is not a reward for the good things we have done, so none of us can boast about it. for we are God's masterpiece. He has created us anew in Christ Jesus, so we can do the good things he planned for us long ago." (Ephesians 2:8-10).

God Is In Love with People

This brings me to one of the biggest surprises in my life. That was the day it dawned on me how incredibly much God loves people. The longer I live, the less I understand it. If the people God loved were perfect people, or if they had earned it in some way, it would make sense. If they were uncommonly talented, wealthy, beautiful, witty, useful to God or to the world, or brilliant, I could understand it. God does not seem to realize that these should be the most legitimate reasons for him to love people. Why would God love rebels, most of whom don't even acknowledge that he exists and created them? God even loves people who *hate* him and persecute his followers! Even worse, God extends his love to drug addicts, adulterers, pedophiles, thieves, liars, murderers, wife beaters, child abusers, the mentally defective, and even people who shake their fists at him! His reasons for loving people are incomprehensible to us.

Wouldn't it be better if God used his power to make everyone live superb, happy lives for seventy or one hundred years? Wouldn't we be happier if he forcefully inserted into every heart tolerance, happiness, joy, and love? Wouldn't those be the kind of people he would choose to adopt into his family?

Several years ago, Becki and I were driving our car home from the dedication of a new village clinic. The sun was blazing, the humidity was oppressive, and we had our windows tightly closed to keep leaves, bugs, and moisture from invading our heavenly, air-conditioned space.

We drove into a pygmy village, and a little man whom I recognized waved for me to stop. Francis was the church elder for about twenty Christians from the village, and he smiled broadly as I slowed to a stop. I lowered the window but kept the motor running and the A/C fan at full power. His head came up to the bottom of the car window, so I had to lean out to talk with him.

We exchanged greetings and handshakes, and I asked him how things were going. He replied that everything was great, but his face and body language told me otherwise. When I asked him what was wrong, he told me there was a sick woman at the far end of the village that he wanted me to see.

"What's her problem?" I asked, resistance showing in my voice. He explained that the woman was coughing a lot and getting weaker by the day. I thought of tuberculosis, a disease that is ravaging rural Africa. I said firmly, "She needs to come to the hospital so one of our doctors can examine her, get a chest X-ray, check out her sputum for TB, and treat her." I didn't say it, but I thought to myself that even breathing the air near her would be a really bad idea.

Francis frowned and shook his head. "I'm worried about her, Doctor. Please, just come with me and see her for yourself." He started walking down the road, certain that I would follow. I rolled my eyes at Becki inside the car to let her know what I thought and explained that I would be gone for a few minutes. The two of us trudged towards the end of the village while other villagers stepped out of their bark and thatch homes to watch. At least twenty pairs of pygmy eyes solemnly followed our steps to the last bark hut in the village.

The hut was about eight feet square and five feet high, so even after I ducked through the low door I could not stand fully upright without my head brushing the thatched roof. A woman who looked at least seventy years old emerged shakily from a tiny bedroom. Her hands trembled as she tied a dirty piece of cloth around her frail chest and body. She might have weighed forty pounds dripping wet. Every few seconds, she coughed, wetly. I could feel the germs entering my lungs with every breath. She was dying, a pathetic specimen of humanity, with absolutely nothing left to offer the world but her disease.

"This is my aunt," Francis said. "Her husband died last month and she's been sick since." My glance drifted over to her low bed made of parallel sticks tied together with vines. I couldn't even imagine what it would feel like to sleep on such a miserable pallet. Her single possession—other than the rag she had tied around herself, was a blackened aluminum pot sitting on a smoking fire in the middle of the floor. It occurred to me that if it weren't for Francis she might be one of the poorest creatures on the planet.

"She needs to come to the hospital, Francis," I repeated, anxious to remove myself from the cloud of corruption hovering in the air. He frowned and shook his head.

"She has no money, Doctor. Can't you give her some medicine to take here?" My irritation flared. "Francis, I have nothing in my car to treat her with. All our medicines are at the hospital, and we need to confirm her diagnosis and supervise her treatment. If you bring her, I will pay her bill! All right?" I couldn't believe how generous I was being.

Something was still bothering Francis, but he finally sighed and said okay. Minutes later, I was purging my lungs with clean air from the car's air conditioner and whipping down the road in our lovely SUV.

When we got back home, I let my colleague from the medical service know that an old woman would be coming within the next day or two with probable tuberculosis, and that my wife and I would pay her bill. This produced a well-deserved murmur of approval.

The week came to an end and the woman did not appear. When my colleague asked me about her, I was surprised. I told her I didn't know why she hadn't come. Privately, I thought to myself, *There you go. You try to help someone and they ignore your advice.* For some reason, though, I was troubled.

That evening I was talking to my wife about the case and a strange question popped into my mind: "How was the old woman supposed to get to the hospital?" I had been in such a hurry to get away I had failed to think of how she would travel the twenty-five miles to the hospital. She couldn't have walked that distance, though Francis wouldn't have thought twice about it, and Francis wouldn't have had the money to pay for her to travel in a bush taxi with a relative. Stricken about my oversight, I quickly put money in an envelope, addressed it to Francis with a note, and handed it to someone traveling in his direction. A day later he arrived with the old woman in tow.

To my surprise she turned out to have pneumonia, not tuberculosis. With proper care, she rapidly regained her strength and weight. After she filled out, she didn't look nearly so old. She turned out to be in her 50s, not in her 70s. Best of all, thanks to Francis's efforts and the loving care she received at the hospital, she invited Christ into her life! I was humbled and ashamed at the coldness of my heart, and at how little I really understood God's boundless love for lost people.

As I reflected on the way things turned out, the question came to mind, "Why would God want somebody like that?" In our world of billionaires, geniuses, artists, and corporate presidents, she is a nobody. She has nothing to offer the world. The only way she could be materially poorer would be if someone stole her cooking pot. When God sent me to meet her, she was sick, old, weak, ugly, uneducated, and of no use to even her immediate family. None of those things mattered to God. He wanted her, loved her, and prodded and pushed me until I helped her. Then he drew her to himself.

I have seen it happen enough to know that God is passionately in love with people. It is one of the most mystifying and wonderful facets of his personality. Not only that, he wants those of us who already know and love him to help him find more of these sons and daughters so he can adopt as many of them as possible into his family.

The Apostle Paul wrote in Ephesians 3:18-19, "And may you have the power to understand, as all God's people should, how wide, how long, how high, and how deep his love is. May you experience the love of Christ, though it is too great to understand fully. Then you will be made complete with all the fullness of life and power that comes from God."

Conclusion

Jesus told a Pharisee in Mark 12:30-31 that the greatest of the commandments that He had given to Moses was the first one: "And you must love the Lord your God with all your heart, and all your soul, all your mind, and all your strength. The second is equally important: "'Love your neighbor as yourself.' No other commandment is greater than these.'" If we are sincere followers of Jesus, then we must love people and show compassion to them whether they are sick, poor, ugly, and sinful, or healthy, beautiful, wealthy, or our enemies.

The last commandment Jesus gave to his disciples is found in Matthew 28:18-20a: "'I have been given all authority in heaven and on earth. Therefore, go and make disciples of all the nations, baptizing them in the name of the Father and the Son and the Holy Spirit. Teach these new disciples to obey all the commandments I have given you'".

Many who call themselves Christians today have chosen to follow one or two of the three commandments Jesus gave to his disciples, leaving out the ones they find to be inconvenient. Only when we obey all three of these commandments will we be compassionate the way God is compassionate. If we truly love our heavenly father with all of our heart, soul, mind and strength, then we will also love those whom he loves, and we will love them enough to go to the ends of the Earth to find them, help them, and introduce them to Jesus, no matter how hard it is, no matter how costly it turns out to be.

In the next chapter we will look at an area of compassion that Western Christians choose to ignore—despite the fact that it represented a significant portion of Jesus' ministry and teaching.

Chapter 9

HEALING THE SPIRITUALLY OPPRESSED

"But if I am casting out demons by the Spirit of God,
then the Kingdom of God has arrived among you."

Matthew 12:28

Worrisome Questions

Has the Kingdom of God arrived among us yet? Of all the works that Jesus performed during his brief but powerful ministry on Earth, delivering the spiritually oppressed is the least discussed and emulated. Why is that? This part of Jesus' ministry was not performed in secret, but in public, and is openly and frequently described in the New Testament, as evidenced in the passages below:

- *"Heal the sick, raise the dead, cure those with leprosy, and cast out demons" (Matthew 10:8a).*

- *So the disciples went out, telling everyone they met to repent of their sins and turn to God. And they cast out many demons and healed many sick people, anointing them with olive oil (Mark 6:12-13).*

- *John said to Jesus, "Teacher, we saw someone using your name to cast out demons, but we told him to stop because he wasn't in our group." "Don't stop him!" Jesus said. "No one who performs a miracle in my name will soon be able to speak evil of me. Anyone who is not against us is for us"*
  (Mark 9:38-39).

Wayne Gudem writes in *Systematic Theology*, "Demon posses-sion is a misleading phrase found in some English translations of the Bible that seems to suggest that a person's will is completely dominated by a demon. The Greek term 'daimonizomai' is better translated 'under demonic influence,' which could range from mild to strong influence or attack."[34]

My review of an online list of thirty different English translations of the Bible only confirmed that the terms "drove out" and "cast out" were the most frequently used, and the terms used by the rest were similar: "expelled," "put out," "forced out," and "sent packing." It would appear that not all translation scholars are in agreement with Gudem.

Nevertheless, did Jesus really mean for us to deliver people from oppressing demons? Healing the sick and curing leprosy seem safe enough, but should we mess with demons? Should intelligent and educated people like us be even talking about this subject? Didn't God intend for this ministry to disappear with the ascension of Jesus and the death of the apostles? Shouldn't we just refer people who act strangely to the psychiatrists and psychologists and encourage the Church not to meddle in something it doesn't understand?
Does God *really* intend for his followers to perform these kinds of miracles today?

The Legacy of Witch Hunts

It is generally agreed that the epicenter of witch-hunts took place between the 1520s and the 1640s. Rodney Stark, the author of *For the Glory of God* wrote:

> *The frequency and intensity of witch-hunting will have been highest when (1) serious efforts were made to suppress magic and sorcery, and there was a high probability that Satanism would be imputed to such activities, and (2) there was substantial conflict among religious groups representing credible threats to one another's institutional power, causing the withdrawal of tolerance for religious nonconformity, and (3) weak central ecclesiastical and/or political governance prevented "national" elites from curtailing local enthusiasm.*[35]

Starke documents that it was neither the humanists nor the rise of science that brought witch-hunts in Western Europe to an end, though humanists and scientists voiced their disapproval after the practice had already come to an end. Rather, "it was deeply committed and well-trained Scholastics, responding to the evidence of their senses, who stripped it of its evidential basis,"[36] and they did so when speaking against witch-hunts took considerable courage.

One of the most notable of these scholastics was the Catholic inquisitor Francisco Vaca, who after being sent in 1549 by the Spanish Church *Suprema* to investigate a witch-burning episode in Barcelona, wrote a powerful indictment against the practice that significantly influenced the course of the Spanish Inquisition. Vaca was one of the first to decry the execution of so-called "witches" on the basis of hearsay, and to call for reform.[37]

It is reasonable to assume that Western churches shied away from the ministry of deliverance as a result of this dark period of church history.

Witch-hunts are not limited to Christian cultures, but to sudden outpourings of intolerance. In May 2010, three Christian men in a village in southern Gabon were seized by animistic villagers and tortured by fire in an effort to force them to confess to practicing sorcery and witchcraft against the rest of the village. The incident began after twenty young men ingested significant amounts of a traditional, hallucinogenic drug called *Iboga*, a rite of passage to the Bwiti religion. Under the influence of this drug, several of the initiates claimed that they saw a destroying spirit rise out of the Protestant church in the center of village. They claimed that the spirit was angry because someone had buried its skull in the ground in front of one of the church's doors. This claim turned the group into a frenzied a mob that dug deep holes in front of the church's two entrances. After several hours of digging the young men discovered a one-inch square piece of bone, which they did not allow anyone else to examine. Encouraged by their finding, the young men broke into the pastor's house and bound his wrists and feet with electrical wire. When a church elder and an elderly widower objected, the mob declared them accomplices and tied them up as well.

By this time every inhabitant of the village had gathered to see what would happen. The two young men who claimed to have seen the spirit proceeded to pour kerosene over the accused men, soaking their clothes. Only the intervention by one of the village chiefs prevented them from lighting the men's clothes on fire. Nevertheless, the chief permitted the young men to pour additional kerosene over the men's feet and burn their feet. The mob did this three or four times before running out of kerosene.

The three victims screamed in agony until they were exhausted, and all three refused to confess to sorcery and witchcraft against the village. This so enraged the two leaders of the mob that they threatened to shoot the pastor with a shotgun. He replied that he was ready to die, rather than confess to something he did not do, and the other two said the same thing. At that point the leaders brought burning pitch torches and held them to the bottom of the victims' feet until they passed out, eventually producing third-degree burns. The entire incident lasted for more than four hours. Eventually the crowd tired of the spectacle, thinned and dissipated. Without spectators, the young men left the scene, leaving their tied victims on the ground. Groaning and weeping, the three men dragged themselves home in the dark, still bound.

I know the story is true because I interviewed the pastor of the church and one of the other injured men after they were brought to our hospital five days later. Once we had removed the dead skin from their feet and dressed them, I drove twenty-five miles to the village and found the third man lying in his house waiting to die. He was a widower and had no family member to help him. His blackened feet were covered with flies, and he had neither food nor water within reach.

Before I left the village, several Christians came out of hiding and showed me the spot where their friends had been tortured in the center of the village. The ground was still stained with kerosene and ashes. The police later came and completed their own investigation. They put out an arrest warrant for five of the leaders and managed to capture two of them, but the other three fled into the forest and months later were still in hiding.

The injured men were hospitalized for two months and required multiple skin grafts to their feet before they could walk again. Hundreds of Christians sent money and brought food, and eventually all three recovered and returned to their village.

This story was featured with photos in the June 1, 2011, issue of *aLife* (Alliance Life), an official publication of the Christian and Missionary Alliance. As in the past, witch-hunting is part of many societies, including animistic cultures. It is never been a prominent feature of Christian history.

What Can Demons Do to Humans?

Most Westerners doubt biblical descriptions of the spirit world, though our culture can be astonishingly fanciful about extraterrestrials. Films like *Poltergeist* are designed for entertainment, not to convince, and are not taken seriously. I've met not a few followers of Jesus in American churches who doubt that the spirits described in the Bible and in animistic cultures are a threat to their faith. Their sentiments about deliverance mirror the dark films that our society has produced about the Catholic church's history of exorcisms, making those who deliver people from demons to be criminals or Christians from the lunatic fringe.

Many of us today consider ourselves to be more knowledgeable about the world than the simple, uneducated peasants who walked the earth in Jesus' time. We postulate that Jesus referred to as demonization in his day must have been schizophrenia, bipolar disease, manic depression, or some other well-known aberrance. Thanks to our expanding understanding about human psychology, brain physiology, and central nervous system pathology, we are quite willing to sweep the subject of demonism under the rug.

Today's Christians may in fact know more about the world and about science than the disciples of Jesus did, but their biblical knowledge about demons is significantly less. Only rarely have I heard American Christians talk about the ministry of deliverance—usually in hushed tones. I have never heard a public sermon on the subject. As I was writing this book, several close friends advised me to leave the subject alone, since it could lead to ridicule and ostracism. Since I have felt led by God to write about it anyway, I would strongly encourage you to read this chapter to the end.

In his book, *The Unseen Face of Islam*, Bill Musk writes:

The very view of reality that gives rise to the beliefs and practices of ordinary Muslims is in many respects far closer to the biblical one than to the [Western] missionary's own mechanistic, scientific worldview. If the Western believer ever comes to be faced with the details of folk Islamic belief and practice, is he able to deal with those phenomena as real entities? Or does he view them as invalid, because his worldview claims that there are no such things as jinn [evil spirits], quarinat *[a spirit double of a human being], or zodiacal influences? Perhaps he sees the ordinary Muslim as "primitive;" after all, sickness is explicable simply by germs, not by the evil eye or sorcery. Will his ensuing activity be one of spiritual power encounter or Western education? For too long, it would seem, in Christian witness among Muslims, there has been no power encounter because there have been no power bearers.*[38]

The Bible teaches us that sometime before or during the creation of the world, God created the angels, including a powerful angel called Lucifer. After he rebelled against God his name was changed to "Satan," which is the Hebrew word for adversary. This is an accurate description of the role he plays as he opposes God and his people. Somewhere between Genesis 1:31 and Genesis 3:1 there appears to have been a rebellion in the angelic world. Revelation 12:7-9 describes this event: "Then there was war in heaven. Michael and his angels fought against the dragon and his angels. And the dragon lost the battle, and he and his angels were forced out of heaven. This great dragon—the ancient serpent called the devil, or Satan, the one deceiving the whole world—was thrown down to the earth with all his angels." Ever since the expulsion of these rebellious spiritual beings from heaven, the Bible refers to them as "evil spirits" or "demons."

Vampires and Demon Gods

My wife trained Christian nursing students at our hospital in Central Africa for thirty years. One day, a student from a nearby tribe known for its worship of a demon spirits, including a powerful demon-God called "Bwiti," came to her with a startling question: could he invite a traditional healer from his village to come into the orthopedic ward to call a demon spirit back into a patient who had recently been hospitalized and put in traction because of serious fractures of his legs?

Now part of Bwiti worship requires that parents invoke the demon god when a child is born and ask him to send one of his "good spirits" to protect their child. People who practice this religion believe that Bwiti sends a spirit to inhabit their child protect him until he grows old and dies. They believe that as long as that resident spirit is happy, their child will be protected from other, more evil spirits and from intentional sorcery practiced against him by enemies inside and outside of the family.

The followers of Bwiti spend much of their time taking care not to offend their resident spirits, because if a resident spirit is angered there is a danger that he will go *en vampire*. Loosely translated, this means that the spirit will leave the person it inhabits, exposing the host to dangerous attacks by other spirits. Worse yet, the angered spirit will now free to fly around and harm other people in the household or village. Sudden illness, accidents, or misfortune in a family or village inevitably raise the suspicion that someone's resident spirit is loose and *en vampire*. The bible does not teach this, but the followers of Bwiti believe it without question.

Offenses that anger spirits are varied, but include being away from one's village too long, failing to consult ancestral spirits that hang around the village, speaking unkindly about a person who died, seeking modern medical treatment without the traditional healer's blessing, and getting too involved with Christians. The list of possible offenses is quite long and can be conveniently enlarged by the traditional healer.

My wife's student explained that it was urgent he call the traditional healer to come, because without his intervention his friend's fractures would not heal and the renegade spirits might attack other patients in the orthopedic ward.

The idea of inviting a traditional healer come to the hospital with his leopard skin, incense, spirit bells, and chants was startling enough, but that the suggestion came from a student who openly confessed his love for Christ was equally disturbing. Somehow the student had attended church for years without understanding that Jesus is diametrically opposed to the practice of invoking spirits to come *into* people's bodies and minds!

Later that week the hospital chaplain intervened and explained the scriptures to the student and his injured friend. The young student prayed for forgiveness and declared his faith in Christ, but his cousin declined the chaplain's offer of help, though he did eventually recover from his fractures without complications. Happily, none of the other patients in the ward suffered any complications either!

If someone asked you for help against a tormenting demon, would you have the biblical knowledge and the faith to throw out the demon in the power and name of Jesus? Before you say yes, we need to look at several other challenges to the ministry of deliverance.

Psychiatric Illness vs. Demon Possession

As we have already noted, most people in the West do not believe in demons, including many Christians. Some link the idea of demons and demonization to the witch-hunts in Europe and North America, rather than to the stories of Jesus casting out demons in the gospels. A likely reason for this is the widening impact of psychiatry and psychology in our culture over the past one hundred forty years. Wilhelm Wundt is credited with establishing the field of psychology as a scientific discipline in 1879. Today, Americans are spending over $270 billion a year on mental health services.

I want to make clear that I do not doubt the reality of psychiatric illness. The observation that people with schizophrenia often report hearing or seeing terrifying spiritual beings does not prove that demons don't exist. It might indicate that people with certain psychiatric illnesses are more sensitive to the presence of demons and are susceptible to their influence, but the bible does not provide an answer about this. Psychiatric diseases exist and affect millions of people. We should be thankful that God in his mercy has allowed researchers to understand more and more about the workings of the brain, and to discover powerful medications to help millions of people. In the same way, counseling by trained psychologists has helped many in our churches who suffer from less severe behavioral disorders.

Because of its successes—its failures are rarely reported—the influence of psychiatry and psychology has grown enormously. These two disciplines have become so influential in some American churches that at times one wonders if psychology has replaced the Word of God as the Church's primary authority.

According to Jesus, many of the people in his day whom we would call "psychotic" or "epileptic" were in fact parasitized by these ancient, evil, spiritual beings the bible calls "demons." When Jesus commanded demons to leave a person's body, they obeyed him and the people who had been afflicted were immediately healed. These spirits knew who Jesus was and were deeply afraid of him.

"So Jesus healed many people who were sick with various demons, and he cast out many demons. But because the demons knew who he was, he did not allow them to speak" (Mark 1:34).

Jesus never claimed that all disease was caused by demons, and in fact, distinguished the conditions caused by demons from other illnesses, including infections (leprosy) and congenital conditions (blindness and lameness from birth). He taught his disciples that demons were morally corrupt beings that were under the command of Satan and that if they were allowed to dominate a human being they would take over and invite others of their kind to join them (Matthew 12:43-45). The disciples saw Jesus deliver countless people whose personalities and actions were under the control of demons, some to the point of madness.

One such person is described by Luke, the physician:

So they arrived in the region of the Gerasenes. As Jesus was climbing out of the boat, a man who was possessed by demons came out to meet him. For a long time he had been homeless and naked, living in a cemetery outside the town. As soon as he saw Jesus, he shrieked and fell down in front of him. Then he screamed, "Why are you interfering with me, Jesus, Son of the Most High God? Please, I beg you, don't torture me!" For Jesus had already commanded the evil spirit to come out of him. This spirit had often taken control of the man. Even when he was placed under guard and put in chains and shackles, he simply broke them and rushed out into the wilderness, completely under the demon's power.

Jesus demanded, "What is your name?"

"Legion," he replied, for he was filled with many demons. The demons kept begging Jesus not to send them into the bottomless pit. There happened to be a large herd of pigs feeding on the hillside nearby, and the demons begged him to let them enter into the pigs. So Jesus gave them permission. Then the demons came

out of the man and entered the pigs, and the entire herd plunged down the steep hillside into the lake and drowned.

When the herdsmen saw it, they fled to the nearby town and the surrounding countryside, spreading the news as they ran. People rushed out to see what had happened. A crowd soon gathered around Jesus, and they saw the man who had been freed from the demons. He was sitting at Jesus' feet, fully clothed and perfectly sane, and they were all afraid. Then those who had seen what happened told the others how the demon-possessed man had been healed. And all the people in the region of the Gerasenes begged Jesus to go away and leave them alone, for a great wave of fear swept over them.

So Jesus returned to the boat and left, crossing back to the other side of the lake. The man who had been freed from the demons begged to go with him. But Jesus sent him home saying, "No, go back to your family, and tell them everything God has done for you." So he went all through the town proclaiming the great things Jesus had done for him (Luke 8:26-39).

This is perhaps the clearest example of how demons are able to take control over human beings and divert their functions for their own use and pleasure, all the while destroying them. This is similar to the action of intestinal parasites, only they can be killed by medicines. Demons cannot be removed with mind-altering drugs, electroshock therapy, or even psychotherapy. They can only be forced out by a greater spiritual power than themselves.

Jesus said to his critics, "But if I am casting out demons by the Spirit of God, then the Kingdom of God has arrived among you. For who is powerful enough to enter the house of a strong man like Satan and plunder his goods? Only someone even stronger—someone who could tie him up and then plunder his house" (Matthew 28-29).

I understand very well that this is wild-sounding stuff to tender Western ears, even to those who grew up reading the New Testament. But the unvarnished truth is that casting out demons was a major part of Jesus' ministry. Why should his followers ignore it today? In Matthew 10:1, Jesus gave his disciples the power and authority to do what he did: "Jesus called his twelve disciples together and gave them authority to cast out evil spirits and to heal every kind of disease and illness."

I was present at our hospital in December of 2006 when a policeman from the neighboring town of Ndende brought his eleven-year-old daughter to our hospital. The story he told us was that two days earlier his daughter had suddenly stopped talking and walking, and seemed dazed. Fearing that she had been poisoned, her parents rushed her to the local hospital. The doctor who examined her could not find any signs of trauma or food poisoning. Because she had no fever or other medical symptoms, he released her with the recommendation that her family take her to see a traditional healer. In other words, he thought an evil spirit was causing her strange behavior.

The next morning the girl was still dazed, but was able to walk stiffly. She could not speak and would not eat. Her father went to his boss and asked for a few days off so he could take his daughter to consult a "healer" in a village in the forest. Because the police chief was a Christian, he urged his officer to forget the healer and take his daughter to our hospital.

The officer followed his boss's advice and several hours later arrived at our hospital. The nurses receiving them said the girl climbed out of the car slowly and shuffled into the emergency department like a zombie. One of our doctors checked her over and eventually concluded that she did not have a medical problem. He called Pastor Pascal, our chaplain, who after listening to the whole story invited the girl and her father into his office and seated them.

Pascal prayed first, then asked the girl to describe what had happened to her. She seemed to hear him but looked at him without replying. Pascal opened his Bible and read aloud a passage from Romans 8:38: "And I am convinced that nothing can ever separate us from God's love. Neither death nor life, neither angels nor demons, neither our fears for today nor our worries for tomorrow—not even the powers of hell can separate us from God's love."

The girl suddenly let out a shriek, and her father jumped to his feet. Pascal turned to the girl and calmly said to the spirit controlling her, "You evil spirit, be quiet, in the name of Jesus!" He then asked the girl again what had happened to her.

After a moment, she replied in her own voice and said, "I can't talk with that man over there." The only two men in the room were Pascal and her father, but she was staring fearfully at an empty chair in the far corner of the room. Pascal looked at the chair and asked her, "That one over there?" She nodded.

Pascal looked hard at the empty chair and said, "You evil spirit, in Jesus' name, get out of my office!" The girl's father watched in astonishment as his daughter watched something that seemed to move across the room and out the closed office door, though neither he nor Pastor Pascal could see anything. Immediately, the girl lost her fear and relaxed.

Pascal again read the passage of scripture in Romans 8. After he finished, the girl said, "Amen!" Since she now seemed almost normal, Pascal briefly explained the gospel to her. Then he asked her if she wanted to invite Jesus into her heart so Jesus could protect her and be her Heavenly Father. She said yes without hesitation, and guided by Pascal, prayed a simple prayer of repentance and faith in Jesus.

After the girl prayed it was as though someone had unlocked her tongue. She talked non-stop! She explained how the day before she had been sitting in her room when a heavy darkness suddenly came over her. She had not had a fight with her mother and nothing unusual had happened to her, but after the darkness came over her, she could hear her mother and father speaking, but couldn't see anything. She couldn't cry out for help, and she couldn't move. It was as if she had been pushed into a dark hole. She was terrified and didn't know what to do. Hours later she fell asleep. The next morning when she woke up she was able to see again and could move around, but her limbs were heavy. It took a great effort to stand up and walk. It was then that she saw what she described as "that evil man." He was big, ugly, and threatened to hurt her if she did not do what he told her. She said she had never seen him before. He followed her everywhere, though her parents couldn't see him.

Those of us trained in psychiatry or psychology would be strongly tempted at this point in the story to interrupt with the explanation that this young girl was having a psychotic episode with hallucinations, and our solution would be to medicate her. Pascal, however, spent the next forty-five minutes explaining to her in simple language what the Bible says about demons, how someone who consults the spirits or other actions can open a door for them to interfere in their families or in their own lives, and how Jesus gave his followers authority over demons. The girl wanted to see these scriptures for herself, so Pascal gave her his open Bible and had her read what Jesus said. When he asked the girl's father if he wanted to receive Christ into his life he replied, "Almost, but not now." Pascal suspected that he had probably been involved in consulting a witch doctor, though he denied it.

Before they left, Pascal turned to the girl and asked her, "Now, did I touch you?" She shook her head. "Did I shout to make the man leave?" She shook her head again. "What did I do?"

"You just told him to leave in the name of Jesus," she said.

"That's what you must do if you ever see that man again," Pascal told her. "It was Jesus who delivered you from this evil spirit. From now on you need to stay close to Jesus and not be afraid." The girl left smiling, holding her father's hand. That was several years ago, and she has remained a normal child.

Now *that* is God's kind of mercy in action!

Anyone involved in this ministry needs training, experience, and discernment—much more than I can provide in this brief chapter. But an important first step to helping people with spiritual oppression is to believe that what Jesus taught his disciples about demon possession is true! The temptation for Christian professionals is to replace Jesus' diagnoses of demonic disease with the new, modern diseases of schizophrenia, bipolar states, and other various psychoses that psychiatrists and psychologists describe. These all have their place, but if the conditions Jesus called "demonic" were caused by childhood traumas and malfunctioning brain cells, wouldn't God the Son have known the difference? If Jesus were continuously present in his world from the moment of creation, would he not have known this when he walked the earth in a human body? What makes us think that we are more qualified to describe what is happening inside human beings who behave abnormally than God the Son, the one who created them? We were not even *there* when he created the first humans! We can understand why his disciples might have been confused by these things, but why would God's Son be confused by them? And if Jesus' teachings on this subject are no longer true, why are Christians in other countries who have faith in God able to dramatically and completely deliver those who are afflicted from the power of demons in exactly the same way that Jesus did, and with the same dramatic results?

The gospel writers make it clear that the spirits Jesus threw out of people were not just the babblings of deranged minds, but intelligent beings with distinct personalities. Here are just a few of Jesus' statements about evil spirits:

- *"And whenever those possessed by evil spirits caught sight of him, the spirits would throw them to the ground in front of him shrieking, 'You are the Son of God!' But Jesus sternly commanded the spirits not to reveal who he was"* *(Mark 3:11-12).*

- *"Then the evil spirits begged him again and again not to send them to some distant place" (Mark 5:10).*

- *"Once when he was in the synagogue, a man possessed by a demon—an evil spirit—began shouting at Jesus. 'Go away! Why are you interfering with us, Jesus of Nazareth? Have you come to destroy us? I know who you are—the Holy One sent from God!' Jesus cut him short. 'Be quiet! Come out of the man,' he ordered. At that, the demon threw the man to the floor as the crowd watched; then it came out of him without hurting him further" (Luke 4:33-35).*

Is Conversion Enough?

There are those who would have us believe that the preaching of the gospel to people who are demonized is all that is needed; that once a person comes to Christ he will *automatically* be delivered from the power of any and all evil spirits that gained access to his personality and mind in the preceding years or decades. That may be true for many, but I know from experience that it is not true for everyone.

Some of you may be troubled about the idea of asking a person who is controlled by demons to invite Christ into his heart before commanding these demons to leave. How can the Spirit of God inhabit the same human spirit as a demon? This is similar to the question the apostle Paul asks in 2 Corinthians 6:14-15: "How can righteousness be a partner with wickedness? How can light live with darkness? What harmony can there be between Christ and the devil?" While I can accept without question that God will never partner with demons, I would humbly reply that the apostle Paul was not specifically talking in this passage about the issue of Christians being oppressed by demons.

To those who would say that it is impossible for a demon-controlled person to become a Christian before he or she is delivered because the Holy Spirit will not share a person's spirit with demons, I would simply point out that we do not know all that much about how people come to faith in Christ, or at what exact point God's Spirit moves in. Can we not simply agree to leave these details up to God? Only God knows what really happens when a person who is controlled by demons cries out to Christ in faith for deliverance. Is God in any way hindered by those demons from helping that person find deliverance?

We think in spatial terms, but does God's spirit merge with a human spirit in the same way that a demon controls and oppresses a person? Where in the universe is God not present? In the spatial sense, he upholds and maintains the same universe in which Satan and his demons live and wreak their havoc. God is completely sovereign in the universe, and that sovereignty includes limiting Satan's power and allowing Satan to only do what serves God's ultimate purposes. Humans were designed for the Holy Spirit, not for demons, and where demons use their power to coerce people to evil, the Holy Spirit frees and empowers the human spirit to do what is good and right.

For the average Christian, knowing the right answer to all these questions about who may be delivered and who may not may not be all that important. I certainly do not claim to be an expert in this ministry, though I have participated in and even led a number of deliverances. So if a brother or sister in the faith believes with certainty that only an unbeliever can be delivered from evil spirits and he or she is willing to follow the teachings of Jesus to deliver those who are demon possessed, may God be praised! What is important is that when someone manifests the presence of an evil spirit in their life and asks us to help them, we don't run the other direction, but we help them, trusting in Jesus to help us and guide us.

Conclusion

Demonic possession exists in our day, just as it did in Jesus' day—not only in certain tribes in Africa or Asia, but all over the world and in all societies. If we deny the existence of demonic possession we must also deny the accounts of how Jesus delivered people from demonic power in the four Gospels and the Book of Acts.

For too long we have joked about those who see "a demon behind every tree." In our disdain for the spiritual healing offered by God to those who are tormented by demons, we have over-sold the power of psychology, psychiatry, and the medications God has given us. God's kind of mercy does not ignore demonic enslavement or assume that it can only be cured by counseling and modern medications. By faith in the clear teaching of Jesus, we can recognize demonic enslavement for what it is and in Jesus' name and power, deliver those who are imprisoned.

Jesus never exempted his disciples from carrying out this ministry. The world will mock Christians who use God's power to bring about healing in this way, but if we are followers of Jesus, we must not deny his power in our service to the world. How can we be the light of the world if we hide when demons challenge us? We have already read what the apostle John recorded of Jesus' last command to his disciples: "As the Father has sent me, so I am sending you." Jesus set the example of how we are to follow him, and our mercy *must* also include the miracle of deliverance.[39]

Chapter 10
BEING THE CHURCH

If a church does not reach out to those who suffer
with acts of mercy and with the gospel,
it is no longer the Church of Jesus Christ.

In 2001, I visited SIM-Galmi Hospital, located in south central
Niger on the very southern edge of the Sahara desert. At that
time, the hospital had just one, full-time surgeon, five or six
African and expatriate medical doctors, and about forty Nigerian
nurses. This miniscule team of committed Christians was trying to
cope with a daily flood of four hundred to five hundred desperate
outpatients, while caring for more than one hundred hospitalized
patients. The staff was so overwhelmed that team members regularly
burned out physically or emotionally and returned home. It was not
a place to which many felt called to serve. In spite of that, year after
year this courageous band of Jesus followers struggled to do its best
to help as many as possible, and share the good news of Jesus with
those they helped.

During my second day there, I went to the surgery outpatient
clinic to help. In the space of four hours, a weary surgeon from New
Zealand rounded on sixty hospitalized surgical patients and treated
close to fifty outpatients. One of the outpatients was a seventeen-
year-old girl with typhoid fever whom I will never forget.

Late in the morning, this young woman's husband pushed through the crowd waiting outside the surgeon's office door, carrying his wife in his arms. The nurses directed him to an examining table where he tenderly laid her. She was a Tuareg, a member of a nomadic tribe in the area. Despite her wasted appearance, she was still beautiful. We examined her and quickly ascertained that she had an intestinal perforation, one of the complications of advanced, typhoid fever. The nurses expertly placed an intravenous line and soon fluids and broad-spectrum antibiotics were flowing into her veins. All of this took less than ten minutes. As she stabilized, the surgeon directed the nurses to place her on a gurney and take her directly to the operating room.

There was another visiting surgeon at the hospital that day, and he operated in one operating room while two African surgical nurses operated in the other. Both teams were already operating on other emergency cases, so the young woman would have to wait her turn. The girl's husband followed the gurney out the door, urgency and fear written in every line of his body.

Thirty minutes later, we finished seeing the rest of the surgical outpatients and hurried over to the operating suite to see if we could be of help. We dressed quickly in scrubs and entered the waiting area outside of the operating rooms. The young woman was still waiting her turn. I was surprised that no one was watching over her. As I approached the gurney, I was struck by how still she was. Someone had stopped her IV, so I opened it up again, irritated that anyone would do something so inappropriate. She seemed to be sleeping, her head turned to one side. Then I touched her, and a wave of grief flooded over me. We were too late! She was gone, in the prime of her life, and we had spoken less than twenty words to her, none of which would help her now.

Every time I think about that young woman's terrible and lonely death, the grief of that moment washes over me. It was not anyone's fault, and she might not have survived the surgery. Everyone involved did everything possible, but the hospital was so chronically understaffed that the surgical team could not do everything that was needed. Most tragically of all, not one of us—myself included—had taken the time to tell this young woman about Jesus. We were all too late.

A Solemn Warning

Only days before his death by crucifixion, Jesus gave his disciples this solemn warning, in Matthew 25:31-46:

> *"[W]hen the Son of Man comes in his glory, and all the angels with him, then he will sit upon his glorious throne. All the nations will be gathered in his presence, and he will separate the people as a shepherd separates the sheep from the goats. He will place the sheep at his right hand and the goats at his left.*

> *"Then the King will say to those on his right, 'Come, you who are blessed by my Father, inherit the Kingdom prepared for you from the creation of the world. For I was hungry, and you fed me. I was thirsty, and you gave me a drink. I was a stranger, and you invited me into your home. I was naked, and you gave me clothing. I was sick, and you cared for me. I was in prison, and you visited me.*

> *"Then these righteous ones will reply, 'Lord, when did we ever see you hungry and feed you? Or thirsty and give you something to drink? Or a stranger and show you hospitality? Or naked and give you clothing? When did we ever see you sick or in prison and visit you?'*

"And the King will say, 'I tell you the truth, when you did it to one of the least of these my brothers and sisters, you were doing it to me!'

"Then the King will turn to those on the left and say, 'Away with you, you cursed ones, into the eternal fire prepared for the devil and his demons. For I was hungry, and you didn't feed me. I was thirsty, and you didn't give me a drink. I was a stranger, and you didn't invite me into your home. I was naked, and you didn't give me clothing. I was sick and in prison, and you didn't visit me.'

"Then they will reply, 'Lord, when did we ever see you hungry or thirsty or a stranger or naked or sick or in prison, and not help you?'

"And he will answer, 'I tell you the truth, when you refused to help the least of these my brothers and sisters, you were refusing to help me.'

"And they will go away into eternal punishment, but the righteous will go into eternal life."

I have heard some interesting sermons about this passage that make it sound as if our ticket to heaven is not our faith in Christ and his work on the cross. For example, it appears that we've earned our ticket because we gave water to the thirsty, were hospitable to strangers, gave clothes to the naked, were merciful to the sick and the poor, and visited prisoners. Presumably, the more of these acts of mercy we carry out the greater will be our salvation. Conversely, if we do not do these things, we will earn ourselves a prominent place in hell. Nothing could be further from the truth!

Jesus said to the Pharisees, "Your mistake is that you don't know the Scriptures, and you don't know the power of God" (Matthew 22:29).

A good rule of theology is that all of what God states about a particular subject in the Bible is true, not just the portions we like. Here are just four of many foundational verses about God's requirements for our salvation:

1. *"But to all who believed him and accepted him, he gave the right to become children of God. They are reborn—not with a physical birth resulting from human passion or plan, but a birth that comes from God" – John 1:12-13.*

2. *"If you confess with your mouth that Jesus is Lord and believe in your heart that God raised him from the dead, you will be saved. For it is by believing in your heart that you are made right with God, and it is by confessing with your mouth that you are saved." – Romans 10:9.*

3. *Jesus replied, "I tell you the truth, unless you are born again, you cannot see the Kingdom of God" – John 3:3.*

4. *"Salvation is not a reward for the good things we have done, so none of us can boast about it." – Ephesians 2:9.*

If these statements from the bible are true, then there is no possible way for a person to earn the forgiveness of sins by feeding the hungry, helping the sick, clothing the naked, or visiting prisoners. This should make us ask, "What was Jesus saying to his disciples in Matthew 25?"

A Litmus Test

Jesus was not introducing a new doctrine in Matthew 25, but giving us a "litmus test" to indicate what represents true belief. Litmus is a chemically treated paper that changes color, depending on the acidity of its environment. In the same way, acts of mercy towards others are not a way for a person to earn his way into heaven, but e*vidence that a person has been born again by the Spirit of God.* What Jesus was saying in this passage was that the absence of mercy in someone who openly confesses to be his follower *is evidence that he never received the Spirit of Christ.*

This immediately raises the question, "What makes us think that we can judge another person when the Bible specifically tells us not to?" Jesus said to his disciples, "'Do not judge others, and you will not be judged. Do not condemn others, or it will all come back against you. Forgive others, and you will be forgiven'" (Luke 6:37).

In Matthew 25, Jesus was not encouraging his disciples to judge and condemn others, but to judge *themselves.* If they claimed to be his followers but did not produce the spiritual fruit of mercy, on the Day of Judgment, he would not even recognize that he knew them.

At one time or another, we have been one of those people who were all words and no action, and we have met people like them. Are they Christians? Are we? What about the great humanitarians of our world, most of whom do not confess with their mouths that Jesus is Lord and do not believe in their hearts that God raised him from the dead? (Romans 19:9). Jesus' statement in Matthew 25 seems at first glance to be a poor litmus test for the absence or the presence of God.

John the Baptist agreed with Jesus, and he said in Luke 3:8, "Prove by the way you live that you have repented of your sins and turned to God. Don't just say to each other, 'We're safe, for we are descendants of Abraham.' That means nothing, for I tell you, God can create children of Abraham from these very stones. Even now the ax of God's judgment is poised, ready to sever the roots of the trees. Yes, every tree that does not produce good fruit will be chopped down and thrown into the fire."

This last statement takes my breath away, especially since I like to believe that every person who simply *calls* himself a follower of Jesus is assured a place in heaven. For Jesus, the lack of spiritual fruit, *especially the lack of mercy,* was evidence enough for God to "sever the roots" and pack a pretender of the faith off to the darkest place in the universe. In Matthew 12:33 Jesus said, "A tree is identified by its fruit. If a tree is good, its fruit will be good. If a tree is bad, its fruit will be bad."

This does not mean that our churches need to rush to set up programs that will identify and eliminate the "trees that produce bad fruit" in their midst. It does mean, however, that God has given us a clear guide by which to judge our own hearts and our own churches. It may also mean that we need to use this standard more openly when we choose our leaders.

What these litmus tests detect and signify is whether the Spirit of God is present in our lives. These tests are not about earning our way into heaven. When we encounter a Christian who does not demonstrate mercy in his life, we should call it sin and confront him gently, humbly, but directly, the way that Jesus taught his disciples. The same is true for churches that claim to be spirit-filled but demonstrate little compassion towards those who are suffering around them or who attend their services.

Should a humanitarian who demonstrates mercy in his life be considered a follower of Christ? The biblical answer is "no." If such a person also confesses with his mouth that Jesus Christ is Lord and believes in his heart that Jesus rose from the dead, then we can and should accept him as a fellow believer.

The Merciless Church

The reports from the political violence in Kenya after the disputed presidential election of 2008 are heartbreaking. A friend of mine who was present at a mission hospital in Kenya during the height of the violence wrote the following account:

> Their crime? They are of the wrong tribe and they have been "ethnically cleansed." They have been "flushed." The "tall weeds" have been cut. There are many polite phrases bandied about here that do not hint at the horror of having been burned out of their homes, of being slashed with machetes, of being immolated alive, of having hundreds of rotting corpses in the mortuary which cannot be claimed by their families and tribes because it is not safe to do so.
>
> Yesterday, I went with a team from Kijabe Hospital to the IDP (internally displaced persons) camps near the town of Naivasha. A week ago the shores of one of the beautiful Rift Valley lakes was the scene of the most horrifying clashes of the tribal war. In this predominantly Kikuyu town, if you were Luo (or sometimes Kalenjin) that was sufficient reason for you to die. There was no defense in the fact that you had lived together, worshiped together, worked together or played together. The refugees flocked to the grounds of the national prison and the police station for security. Today thousands are huddled with whatever household goods they could salvage looking at a bleak future. Hard numbers are hard to come by—the best guess is that 6,000 to 10,000 people are in three major camps which blossomed from dry ground over the past week. Those within the camps have

neither shelter from rain nor relief from the burning equatorial sun. Food is scare or non-existent. Blankets are rare and people are wearing multiple layers of whatever clothes they could bring, in an attempt to protect themselves from the chill of the Kenyan highland night. Water is being trucked in but is carefully rationed. Sanitation is woefully inadequate. Until the recent digging of some trench latrines, everyone defecated and urinated where they could find a bit of privacy. This is a public health and social disaster. At the police station, up to 2,000 refugees have overwhelmed the grounds of the little compound. Those most fortunate crawl into the wrecks of old cars being held for evidence in road-traffic accidents, and they are thankful for the shelter.

Eighty percent of Kenyans proclaim themselves Christians. The percentages are relatively equal between the tribes. I can only draw one of two conclusions. One is that Christians are participating in the acts of violence and hatred. The other alternative is that they are being silent—it seems improbable that 80 percent could not squelch the acts of even the most violent 20 percent if they decided to do so."

Where was the Church during these terrible events? There were some wonderfully brave Christians who tried to save their friends, but for the most part, the enormous population of "Christians" in Kenya remained silent, and in too many cases actually participated in the killing. When they were tested, the fruit of mercy was not evident in their lives.

Most of us do little or nothing in our own communities to help the poor or the homeless. Even if our churches have developed programs to reach out to those who are suffering, very few individuals in our churches are willing to serve without pay, let alone volunteer or contribute financially to help others.

Where is the Church when a woman in obstructed labor in Africa comes to an openly Christian hospital and is refused an operation until she or her family can find money to pay? As her contractions slowly kill her unborn child, or as she bleeds to death, "Christian" nurses just yards away ignore her suffering and chatter and laugh with each other—I did not make up these incidents. Where is the evidence of the Spirit of God?

And closer to home, where is the Church when each year a million American unborn babies are destroyed for our convenience, and we shrug our shoulders? Is their blood not on our hands?

Where is the Church when year after year teenage girls are forced to undergo genital mutilation in public ceremonies, and Christians in the community remain silent?

Where are God's people when a teenage boy is refused treatment by a Christian doctor because the family has no money to pay for his treatments, and the doctor—an esteemed member of the local church—is unwilling to relent and give the family time to find the money?

Where is mercy when a missionary or a pastor preaches the gospel for a decade to his congregation, while in the church's shadow there are those living in cardboard houses who have little food, drink unsafe water, and have neither health care or schools? Does God lack for adequate resources? Do these church leaders even ask God to provide resources for these needs? Are these likely to be churches filled with merciful people who reach out to the poor, the hungry, the widow, and the orphan, or are they churches that bring God so much shame that he disavows them?

In Isaiah 1:13-17, God openly challenged his people to repent for their lack of mercy.

"Stop bringing me your meaningless gifts, the incense of your offerings disgusts me! As for your celebrations of the new moon and the Sabbath and your special days for fasting—they are all sinful and false. I want no more of your pious meetings. I hate your new moon celebrations and your annual festivals. They are a burden to me. I cannot stand them! When you lift up your hands in prayer, I will not look. Though you offer me prayers, I will not listen, for your hands are covered with the blood of innocent victims. Wash yourselves and be clean! Get your sins out of my sight. Give up your evils ways. Learn to do good. Seek justice. Help the oppressed. Defend the cause of orphans. Fight for the rights of widows."

In Isaiah 58:7, God cried out against the false piety of His people: "Share your food with the hungry and give shelter to the homeless. Give clothes to those who need them and do not hide from relatives who need your help. Then your salvation will come like the dawn, and your wounds will quickly heal. Your godliness will lead you forward and the glory of the Lord will protect you from behind. Then when you call, the Lord will answer."

Speaking through the prophet Ezekiel in Ezekiel 16:49, God compared his people to the people of Sodom: "Sodom's sins were pride, gluttony, and laziness, while the poor and needy suffered outside her door."

If we take Jesus at His word in Matthew 25:31-46, the church that does not reach out to those who suffer with both material help and the gospel is no longer a church that he cares to call his own.

What kind of church is yours? What kind of mercy does it demonstrate? What kind of mercy is exemplified by your life and work?

The clear teaching of Jesus is that where there is no mercy, there is no holiness either.

Chapter 11

THE HOPE OF THE WORLD

"Look, I am making everything new!" And then he said to me, "Write this down, for what I tell you is trustworthy and true." And he also said, "It is finished! I am the Alpha and the Omega—the Beginning and the End. To all who are thirsty I will give freely from the springs of the water of life. All who are victorious will inherit all these blessings, and I will be their God, and they will be my children."

Revelation 21:5-7

The Impossible Assignment

J esus' final command was an assignment for the Church to extend God's compassion to all the nations of the world, regardless of the cost. His command was so overwhelming that even today, more than two thousand years later, it seems impossible to complete. His command is recorded in all four gospels and in the book of Acts.

The apostle Matthew recorded it this way (Matthew 28:18-20): "I have been given all authority in heaven and on earth. Therefore go and make disciples of all the nations, baptizing them in the name of the Father and the Son and the Holy Spirit. Teach these new disciples to obey all the commands I have given you. And be sure of this: I am with you always, even to the end of the age."

Mark recorded it this way, in Mark 16:15: "Go into all the world and preach the Good News to everyone. Anyone who believes and is baptized will be saved. But anyone who refuses to believe will be condemned."

Luke the physician talked with numerous witnesses and recorded the following: "Yes, it was written long ago that the Messiah would suffer and die and rise from the dead on the third day. It was also written that this message would be proclaimed in the authority of his name to all the nations, beginning in Jerusalem. There is forgiveness of sins for all who repent."

The apostle John wrote in John 20:21: "Peace be with you. As the Father has sent me, so I am sending you."

In Acts 13:47, the Apostle Paul quoted Isaiah 49:6, where the Messiah said, "You will do more than restore the people of Israel to me. I will make you a light to the Gentiles, and you will bring my salvation to the ends of the earth."

Defining the Church's Mission

Some time ago, I attended a conference on AIDS at very large Christian church. The conference lasted three days and featured a number of well-known speakers. The plenary sessions were carefully planned and quite helpful. People came from all over the world to learn and to network with others involved in this ministry of compassion.

During the first day, we heard great preaching and teaching about the need for Christians to practice mercy, especially towards those suffering from HIV/AIDS. We heard dramatic stories illustrating how individuals and churches found creative and beautiful ways to help the suffering. These included repairing the homes of HIV/AIDS patients, paying school fees for their children, transporting them to the doctor for their scheduled or emergency visits, providing nutritious food for the whole family, and making certain that they took their medications regularly and correctly.

The love and mercy provided for these HIV/AIDS patients was uplifting and honoring to God. But by the morning of the second day, I began to sense that something was missing. I mentioned to several colleagues who were attending that there was no mention at all of the need to proclaim Christ to these people, and they agreed. They suggested that perhaps this aspect was being left out because "there is a time and a place for everything," and our first response should be to respond with love to people's felt needs. I couldn't have agreed more with that idea, but then another delegate suggested that perhaps the importance of sharing the good news of Jesus was being deliberately left out because it was "like the water under a ship on the ocean" and was understood by everyone as "essential for the entire effort." Another theorized that proclaiming Christ was being downplayed because there were people from other religions attending who might be offended.

By the third and final day, everyone in our group was troubled that we were hearing almost nothing about the importance of proclaiming Jesus to those helped in practical and loving ways. Our concern turned to dismay when two statements by the organizers were presented as major pillars of their teaching, and without any significant qualifications. The first was that "The hope of the world is the Church." The second was that "It is therefore the responsibility of the church worldwide to conquer the AIDS epidemic!" Both statements were followed by loud and prolonged applause.

I sat without applauding, in the midst of an assenting crowd of nearly three thousand people, simply too stunned for words. I thought, *What Church are we talking about?* The Universal Church of Jesus Christ was being equated to all of the church buildings in one African nation and its declared mission was to conquer AIDS.

If it is true that churches whose only qualification is that they call themselves Christians, then the world is in serious trouble. Add to that the mission to eradicate AIDS, and one has to wonder if Jesus seriously misstated his command to his disciples in Matthew 28:19-20 to make disciples of all nations. If our new mission is to eradicate AIDS, it should follow that our mission must also include the eradication of *all* of the world's major ills, including malaria, resistant tuberculosis, the current round of civil wars, the hatred between Palestinians and Jews, and the endless rapes of thousands of women in eastern Congo. I have no doubt that God has very significant roles for his Church to play as the salt and light of the world, but where did he call on his disciples to focus all of their energies and resources to solve the world's major problems? The last time the Church tried to do that it launched the Crusades to save Jerusalem from the Arabs.

The statement that "the Church is the hope of the world" is true only if the Church is obedient to the commands, teachings, and example of Jesus Christ. Used as a launching pad for projects to eradicate the world of its major ills, it will distract us from our unique and compassionate role of proclaiming Jesus Christ and his gospel to the nations. In our enthusiasm to be merciful and acclaimed by the world through human effort, we risk hijacking God's real plan for the Church.

In the book of Colossians the apostle Paul talks about the importance of the Church, but encourages the Colossian Christians to place their hope in its head, Jesus Christ. In Colossians 1:18 he stated, "Christ is also the head of the church, which is his body." Then in verses 2-4 in the second chapter he wrote that he wanted them to "be encouraged and knit together by strong ties of love. I want them to have complete confidence that they understand God's mysterious plan, which is Christ himself. In him lie hidden all the treasures of wisdom and knowledge" (*emphasis* mine).

In verse 9 of that same chapter Paul writes, "For in *Christ* lives all the fullness of God in a human body" (*emphasis* mine). Never once in the New Testament did Paul infer that ecclesiastical leaders had the right or the authority to change the primary focus of what we call "The Great Commission."

I will grant that God has a great and magnificent work for the Church to accomplish in the world before the return of Jesus. In Matthew 5:14 he stated to his disciples, "You are the light of the world—like a city on a hilltop that cannot be hidden." The list of what churches could give in resources and volunteers to help the world's suffering people is almost limitless. But what is God's priority? Is it not to complete the long overdue mission to carry the gospel of Jesus to every nation and tribe in the world, in a way that proclaims His power combined with our weakness? In accomplishing Christ's mission, we will fulfill the promise of Matthew 24:14, where Jesus said, "And the good news about the Kingdom will be preached throughout the whole world, so that all nations will hear it; *and then the end will come*" (*emphasis* mine).

On the day the gospel is proclaimed to every last tribe and nation on earth, the stage will be set for the return of the world's rightful king. *That* is how God intends his Church to be the hope of the world! The rightful head of the Church, Jesus, is in charge of this great enterprise, and we are his willing and obedient hands and feet.

John the Baptist said about Jesus, "Look! The Lamb of God who takes away the sin of the world!" (John 1:29).

Jesus said of himself in John 3:14, "And as Moses lifted up the bronze snake on a pole in the wilderness, so the Son of Man must be lifted up, so that everyone who believes in him will have eternal life." In John 3:35 he exclaimed, "The Father loves his Son and has put everything into his hands. And anyone who believes in God's Son has eternal life."

In Revelation 1:8, the risen Savior said, "I am the Alpha and the Omega—the beginning and the end. I am the one who is, who always was, and who is still to come—the Almighty one."

It is the Lamb of God who is the hope of the world, and we are his partners in bringing that hope to the broken and the lost. That is why we must tell the sick and the dying, the outcasts and the hungry, the thirsty, naked, homeless, and imprisoned that Jesus loves them and longs to adopt them into his family. Without Jesus, all of our mercy and compassion amounts to nothing.

John Stott wrote the following about a fuller doctrine of the church:

> On the one hand, the church is a "holy" people, called out of the world to belong to God. But on the other it is a "worldly" people, in the sense of being sent back into the world to witness and to serve. Seldom in its long and chequered history has the church remembered or preserved its double identity. Sometimes, in a right emphasis on its "holiness," the church has wrongly withdrawn from the world and become insulated from it. At other times, in a right emphasis on its "worldliness" (i.e. its immersion in the life of the world) the church has wrongly become assimilated to the world's standards and values, and so become contaminated by them. Yet without the preservation of both parts of its identity, the church cannot engage in mission.[40]

The final hope of the world today is not the bride *without* her bridegroom, but *with* her bridegroom! That is why the North American church, with all of her money, armies of middle-class volunteers and organization, cannot be the hope of the world. The hope of the world will forever be Jesus Christ, the risen Lamb of God and head of the Church.

Our focus to complete the mission of mercy that God has given us must not be halted by the disasters that beset the world but energized by them. As we sacrificially help those who suffer, the world will demand that we remain silent about Jesus, but that is something we must never, ever set aside. Instead, out of love we must proclaim Jesus to every person on the planet. We must never give up, never lose hope, and above all, we must never make a deal with the dragon!

If we are to accomplish our mission to the world we will need the presence and power of the Holy Spirit to fill our lives fill our churches, and change our priorities. God has not called us to exhaust ourselves in a futile effort to save the world, but he *has* called us take his light to the world in power, mercy and love, proclaiming Jesus as we go. This is the truest mercy. This is Christian mercy.

END NOTES

1. "What is the *Mission* of the Church?" Kevin DeYoung & Greg Gilbert, Crossway, 2011, p. 22

2. Ibid, pp. 22-26

3. Richard Stearns, *The Hole in Our Gospel*, World Vision, Inc, 2009, p. 238

4. Steve Moore, *Who Is My Neighbor,* NavPress, 2010:58

5. Timothy Lane, Paul Tripp, *Relationships, A Mess Worth Making,* New Growth Press, 2006, 2008:136

6. Christian Buckley and Ryan Dobsen, *Humanitarian Jesus, Social Justice and the Cross,* Moody Publishers 2010, p. 24

7. Laurie Garrett, *The Challenge of Global Health*, Laurie Garrett, Article from Foreign Affairs, January/February 2007, p. 1

8. www.msf.org/msfinternational/

9. www.ifrc.org/what/values

10. Webster's Online Dictionary

11. Rodney Stark, *For the Glory of God,* 2003, Princeton University Press, pp. 147

12. Randall K. O'Banner, Ph.D, *NRL News,* p.18, Jan 2008, Vol. 35, Issue 1

13. Oxford Online Dictionary

14. John Stott, *Issues Facing Christians Today* (HarpurCollinsReligious, 1984, 1990), p. 6

15. Robert Handy, *The Social Gospel in America*, (Oxford University Press, 1966) p. 50

16. John Horsch, *Modern Religious Liberalism,* (Scotsdale, PA.: Fundamental Truth Depot, 1920, 1921), p. 181

17. Steve Corbett and Brian Fikkert,*When Helping Hurts*, (Moody Publishing, 2009), p. 47

18. Ibid, p. 47

19. James F. Engel and William A. Dyrness, *Changing the Mind of Missions: Where Have We Gone Wrong?"* (Downers Grove, Ill.: InterVarsity, 2000), p. 22

20. Brian L. McLaren, *Everything Must Change* (Thomas Nelson, 2007), p. 19

21. Ibid, p. 33

22. Ibid, p. 34

23. Ibid, pp. 79-80

24. Ibid, p. 94

25. Ibid, p. 119

26. John Stott, *Christian Mission in the Modern World* (Intervarsity Press, 1975), pp. 37-38

27. Christian Buckley & Ryan Dobsen, *Humanitarian Jesus, Social Justice and the Cross* (Moody Press, 2010), p. 150.

28. Laurie Garrett, *The Challenge of Global Health*, Article from *Foreign Affairs*, January/February 2007, p. 1

29. Crocker, David W., *The Samaritan Way* (Chalice Press, 2008), p. 33.

30. Ibid, p. 37

31. Matthew 9:22

32. Edwin Lin, Steven Calvano, and Stephen Lowry, *Schwartz's Principles of Surgery,* 8th edition (McGraw-Hill Professional, 2004) Chapter 1, p. 4

33. John Stott, *Christian Mission*, p. 35

34. Wayne Gudem, Systematic Theology, 1994, Intervarsity Press, p. 1239

35. Rodney Stark, *For the Glory of God,* 2003, Princeton University Press:255

36. Ibid, p. 287

37. Ibid, p. 284

38. Bill Musk, *The Unseen Face of Islam* (Monarch Books, Mill Hill, London and Grand Rapids, Michigan, 2003), pp. 227-228

39. For those wishing to learn more, I recommend Dr. Neil Anderson's books, V*ictory Over Darkness,* Regal Books, 1990, and *The Bondage Breaker,* 1990, Harvest House Publishers, both of which present a biblically-based overview of the subject of demon possession and the ministry of deliverance.

40. Stott, *Issues Facing Christians Today,* 1990, p. 24